PHARAOHS AND MORTALS

PHARAOHS AND MORTALS

by TORGNY SÄVE-SÖDERBERGH

Translated from the Swedish by
Richard E. Oldenburg

THE **BOBBS-MERRILL** COMPANY, INC.
A SUBSIDIARY OF HOWARD W. SAMS & CO., INC.
Publishers • INDIANAPOLIS • NEW YORK

Contents

Illustrations

PLATES

Foreword

In a series of radio talks and newspaper articles, I have tried to spread joy and envy—joy by transmitting some of my enthusiasm for the varied aspects of Egyptian culture, envy among those unfortunates whose hobbies are not also their professions.

It is with the same intention that I now issue these sketches of Egyptian culture, somewhat revised, in book form. In general, the style of the verbal presentations has been retained. In the translations, I have not sought philological precision so much as I have tried, in so far as possible, to have the texts convey to the modern reader the same impressions as the original versions conveyed in their own time. This a more literal translation can never accomplish, because of the character of the language and the many special terms which conveyed associations and moods we moderns cannot readily understand or experience.

Many problems are still unsolved, many questions are controversial. What I have wanted to give is my own conception of ancient Egyptian life, based on my studies and those of others, not an account of the current status of research on the subject. Because of the frailties of the material, it is unavoidable that some things should be rather hypothetical, but those which cannot strictly be proved scientifically are in any case highly probable, in terms of the over-all perspective we get from the inexhaustibly rich source materials.

My primary goal has not been to transmit a mass of facts, but rather to seek out the spirit of the time and the individual man of ancient Egypt, as reflected in various situations and milieux, and to understand the shifting cultural life in the context of its own setting and basic assumptions.

Torgny Säve-Söderbergh

FROM EGYPTIAN HISTORY

The dangerous border

For a long time the Sinai desert has been best known to us as a concept from Biblical history, the place where the children of Israel wandered after their flight from Egypt and where Moses received the Ten Commandments. But most recently the Sinai and the neighboring portions of Palestine, particularly the Gaza area, have assumed hideous prominence as a theater of war and a disputed borderland between Egypt and Israel.

If you look back to earlier history, you will find that the Sinai has almost always been prominent in just this sense. It is not surprising when you consider geographic and political circumstances.

Egypt, or rather the habitable part of Egypt—the Nile Valley —can best be characterized as an enormous oasis in the Sahara Desert, a thin belt of arable land surrounded by endless stretches of barren desert which at most can sustain only a few isolated Bedouin tribes.

In ancient times Egypt could be threatened neither from the east nor the west, since no large assemblage could group there for an invasion. The external threat was always concentrated at three points: the southern border; the northwestern border, near Libya, by the sea; and the northeastern border which faced the Sinai and Palestine. The southern threat, from the tribes who lived at the head of the Nile, was comparatively easy to ward off. In Egypt's long history a people from the Sudan succeeded only once in conquering the land. From the northwest—from Libya—the danger was somewhat greater. There, too, however, conditions did not favor the rise of a major competitive power. All the assaults which came from this direction, and there were many, could be thrown back, as they were most recently during World War II.

The real danger from without, before the era of the modern great powers, threatened Egypt not from the south or the northwest, but from the Sinai border.

Even there Egypt was protected by a desert barrier about one hundred twenty miles wide, stretching from Kantara by the present Suez Canal to the Gaza region, now so much in the news, where the land again becomes fertile enough to support an army. In comparison with the deserts east and west of Egypt, this stretch of desert was easy to cross, and this fact alone was enough to make this the dangerous border for Egypt.

It was dangerous to a higher degree, because the lands beyond the border were directly linked to regions with natural resources favoring the rise of great powers which could compete with Egypt and present deadly threats. The Palestine and Syria of ancient times were not in themselves a serious threat to Egypt, but in these lands more distant Eastern powers could assemble great armies. It was on this front that the Egyptians had to battle the Mitanni kingdom, the Hittites, the Assyrians, the Babylonians, and the Persians, to mention only the earliest invaders.

We first encounter the Egyptians on the Sinai peninsula at the time of the pyramids, during the third dynasty, in the twenty-eighth and twenty-seventh centuries before Christ. But it was apparently not to make their borders secure that the Egyptians advanced on the Sinai peninsula; in any case, this was probably not their prime objective. There was then no foreign power which could threaten the Egyptian kingdom, either in the south or the north, and the forays the Egyptians made beyond their natural borders were to find raw materials lacking on Egyptian territory. Above all, they were seeking metals and various beautiful stones. The Sinai is comparatively rich in copper, and this may also explain why the Egyptians established quarries there. But if the testimony of the many inscriptions is to be trusted, the most important item was not copper but a blue semiprecious stone, very probably turquoise.

The extraction of turquoise from the stone quarries near Maghara and Serabit el Khadim, in the southern part of the Sinai peninsula, began during the third dynasty and continued throughout the history of ancient Egypt up until about 1000 B.C.

Quarrying in this area presented great difficutlies. Even the route to the quarries was arduous. We are not quite sure what means of transportation was used, but probably both men and equipment were brought by boat from the present-day Suez region, on the Red Sea coast. The quarries lay a short distance inland from the coast, and while water was available in the mountains where the men worked, there was nothing else. Moreover, the water was bad, and its consumption over a period of time caused stomach troubles. All food had to be brought along and presumably also feed for the pack animals, usually donkeys. And the quantities involved were not small. We have two accounts which give some idea of how many took part in a quarrying expedition. On the first occasion there were 734 men; on the second, 209 men and 284 donkeys. All of them had to be supplied with food and drink for as long as the expedition lasted.

Even this was not all they needed. In the region of the quarries a shrine had been built for the patron goddess of the mines, "Hathor, Ruler of the Turquoise." Like the pious men they were, the Egyptians saw to it that the goddess received her rich tribute during the time of their stay. Here again, the quantities were not small by any means. According to one text, the daily offering included 350 honey breads, 320 white breads, 360 mugs of beer, 60 geese, and 100 mugs of water—and this list is only partially preserved; it probably included still more items.

If copper had been the main concern, we might better understand the great effort and cost expended on the expedition itself and on pleasing the patron goddess Hathor. After all, copper was one of the necessities of life, particularly in a society which still used neither iron nor bronze to any great extent and which made all its metal implements from copper. But the most important product was apparently something as unnecessary as turquoise, which could be used only in jewelry for men and gods and which, moreover, was of such poor quality that it lost its color after a time.

Here we have something to ponder. What we regard as an impractical luxury may be regarded by people with different values and modes of life as something of worth beyond question, as more or less essential. The "luxury," turquoise, must have cost the lives of many Egyptians. Certainly many died on the difficult route to the mines and in the course of their terrible labors, as they dug channels in the mountainsides with primitive implements, under the constant menace of rock slides.

The mines of the Sinai are also interesting from another point of view. The Egyptians were not the only ones who labored there. On the list of those who took part in the expeditions, we often encounter Asians, most commonly from Palestine. That they were not simple mineworkers only is apparent from a couple of texts which refer to such highborn people as, for example, a "brother of the prince of Retenu"—that is to say, of Palestine. Aside from the purely Egyptian inscriptions, there are also twenty-five texts which are not in Egyptian writing. For a long time what kind of writing this was remained a puz-

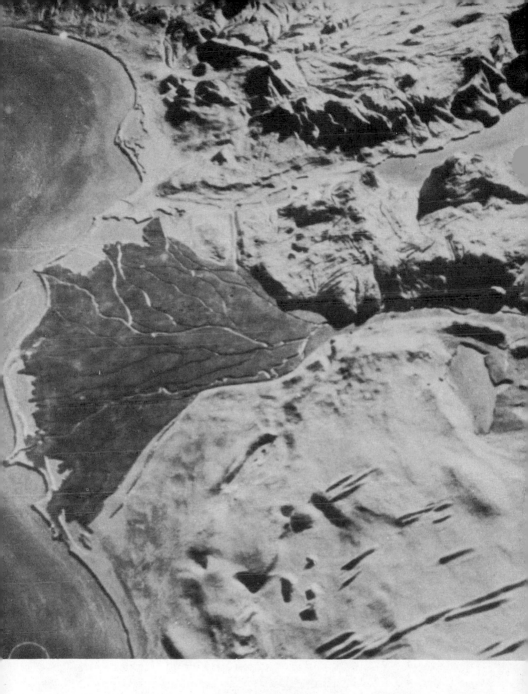

G. Eriksson

Relief model of the Nile River Delta and the Sinai.
From relief map in the Victoria Museum, Uppsala.

Semites on a visit to Egypt. Details from a
painting in Beni Hassan. Nineteenth century B.C.
From Davies, *Ancient Egyptian Painting*.

zle, but eventually it was recognized as the earliest precursor of the Canaanite-Phoenician writing, the first real alphabetical script and the ancestor of the alphabet which we still use today.

Its creation can be traced to the inspiration which the Semites, who worked with the Egyptians in the turquoise mines, derived from their literate and literary co-workers and supervisors. With the hieroglyphics as a starting point, they developed their own writing by simplifying the complicated picture writing into a pure alphabet.

It seems curious that contact with the high culture of Egypt under the inhumanly hard conditions of the Egyptian turquoise mines should have produced one of humanity's greatest achievements in the development of writing.

While contacts here in the mines between the Egyptians and their neighbors in the northeast were usually marked by peaceful co-operation, the same can hardly be said of the region farther north on the Sinai peninsula, near the age-old military route through the desert along the coast of the Mediterranean.

From the earliest historical times, around 3000 B.C., the Egyptians had lively trade relations with Syria. As far as we know, they then used the sea as the less difficult transport route. There is nothing to suggest that they had any difficulties at that time with the inhabitants of Palestine. Not until the twenty-fourth century, toward the end of the pyramid period, do we hear of warlike developments. We are told then that King Pepi I took the field with an army of tens of thousands against "the Asian builders on the sand." Like all the Egyptian troop expeditions—if we believe the Egyptian texts—this one resulted in a glorious victory. The army returned without losses after having laid waste the enemy's land, invested their fortresses, cut down their fig trees and grape vines, and decimated their able-bodied men or led them as captives to Egypt. Despite this triumph, the maneuver had to be repeated no fewer than five times, since the enemy refused to submit, a fact which permits some doubts about the magnitude of the first victory.

This is the first mention of problems of foreign policy in regard to the dangerous frontier in the northeast. Despite all the troop expeditions, the danger remained throughout the final years of the pyramid era. The whole time, the inhabitants of Palestine pressed against the Egyptian border, and no one moved safely in the border region. Under the last king of the pyramid era, Pepi II, an official who had been sent to the Red Sea coast to build a ship for an expedition to Somaliland was slaughtered by roving Semites.

After the death of Pepi II the Egyptian realm was split into small kingdoms, warring against each other. Egypt lost the whole eastern Delta. Only with the utmost difficulty did the Egyptians succeed eventually in driving back the Asian interlopers.

How bad the situation had become is clear from the fact that a Pharaoh of this period thought he had accomplished something remarkable when he managed to restrict the Asians to the plundering of travelers rather than of populous cities. By this feat, he says glowingly, the Asians were scaled down to a plague comparable to crocodiles. To crush them on their home ground was hopeless.

"It is a wretched land that the Asian inhabits," the same Pharaoh tells us. "Water is scarce, trees can barely grow, and the roads are bad in the mountain regions. He never stays in one place, because lack of food sends him wandering about, roaming by foot across the desert. Since time immemorial he has fought against us. He cannot win but neither can he be defeated. He attacks without warning and then slinks away like a thief who will make no stand against troops."

When Egypt was once again united into a powerful state, she roused herself in the northeast. During the so-called Middle Kingdom, the Asians were expelled from the Delta and an effective border barrier was established. Along the present-day course of the Suez Canal was built a long line of fortresses with high watchtowers, where soldiers stood guard day and night to hinder all illegal passage. The region beyond the border was pacified, and the supremacy of the Egyptian king acknowledged —most probably, all the way up to Syria.

But the seesaw game continued. As soon as Egypt was again weakened by internal strife in the 1700s, and the border guard began to slacken, large numbers of Semites wandered back into Egypt. That this was an immigration of major proportions is indicated by a recently uncovered papyrus which lists the members of an apparently average Egyptian household during this period. The servants are for the most part Semites; for every three Egyptians there are four Asians—men, women or children.

Soon we are back in the same situation as before the Middle Kingdom. The entire east Delta fell into the hands of the Asians, and they could no longer be held within these bounds. And one fine day a Semitic people, the Hyksos, sat as rulers on the Egyptian throne. These foreign princes ruled the land for over a hundred years, but in this situation Egypt resorted to its ultimate defense—its remarkable gift for assimilating outside elements. The foreigners soon became wholly Egyptianized and comported themselves in precisely the same manner as the native kings. The majority of the land's inhabitants found themselves quite content with the Semitic Pharaohs.

In the long run, however, the foreigners could not manage the nice feat of holding together the Nile Valley, with its long lines of communication, under a strong central government. Various parts of the country made themselves independent, and finally the last Hyksos ruler and his hangers-on were driven from Egyptian ground by a princely family from Thebes in Upper Egypt.

From this internal strife Egypt emerged as a nation fundamentally changed. Before, the battles had been waged by temporary conscripts, but now professional soldiers took over.

History had taught the Egyptians that if they could not effectively control Palestine, the perennial gateway for attacks on the eastern Delta, they would never know peace in their land. And so begins the great warlike expansion to the north. First, the Egyptians conquered Palestine, but the structure of the rest of the Middle East had so changed that even this was no longer sufficient to ensure peace for Egypt. The Palestinian princes had allied themselves with their colleagues farther north in Syria. Behind them stood a great power, the state of the Mitanni, in the upper portion of the Tigris and Euphrates Valley.

The Egyptians drove farther and farther north, and each pause in this expansion brought on immediate defeats. During the next centuries the battles were no longer fought at the Sinai border. Instead, they billowed back and forth in northern Palestine and southern Syria, first between Mitanni and Egypt, later between the Hittites and the Egyptians. The danger zone had moved northward, and the Egyptians succeeded in holding a buffer beyond the Sinai border.

But even in this situation, Gaza and Sinai were key points, the last line of defense in time of danger. In Gaza a strong Egyptian garrison was maintained; and along the ancient military route through the Sinai desert was built a series of fortified rest points, where the soldiers could get water and provisions. The line of fortifications and border guards along the eastern shore of the Delta were once again set in full operation. We still have a couple of the meticulous journals which were kept here, recording all those who passed in or out across the border. There were messengers, diplomatic envoys, inspectors of the fortifications. Sometimes the entries may read like this:

"A report to my Lord:

"We have now permitted the Asiatic tribes of Edom to pass by the fort, which is in Tjeku [near the present Kantara], which will give them a chance of saving themselves and their herds, by the grace of Pharaoh, who is the sun of every land."

"I have sent, my Lord, a complete list of them and of the days on which they passed the fort."

This text might well serve to illustrate the Biblical story of how Abraham passed into Egypt to live there for some time, since famine was abroad in the land, or of how Joseph's brothers traveled to Egypt to buy grain, "so that they might live and not die."

We also have illustrations of the less agreeable contacts the inhabitants of Palestine had with the Egyptians, who put bailiffs in charge of them, oppressed them with slave labor, and forced them to build for Pharaoh the supply centers Pithom and Raamses, as the second book of Moses tells us.

Raamses was the new capital, which Ramses II raised on the east Delta in the 1200s, to bring the administrative center closer to the battlefields in Syria and Palestine. This city is described in many Egyptian texts. It lay, we are told, where Egypt ended and the foreign lands began. There the chariot troops were gathered, the armies were mustered, all the ships of the fleet had their home base, and the surrounding countryside flowed with milk and honey.

The forced labor of the Israelites is also well documented. Camps for prisoners of war and foreign slave labor are familiar through archeological remnants, texts, and pictures, which show that foreign workers were usually pressed into doing as much of the heavy labor as possible.

Not only foreign peoples had a hard time in this border region. Life was no bed of roses even for the Egyptians, and many homesick sighs have been preserved in texts from soldiers and officials posted to the desert fortresses or the garrison cities. Since the term of such service might last for six years or more—this is mentioned as not at all unusual—one can well understand a complaint like the following:

"Here I am, stuck in Kenkenento [a place name which means, roughly, "plague on the land"]. All the equipment I had with me has disappeared, and all I do is sit and look at the birds and fish a little. The whole time, my eye rests on the Syria road [which led home]. I lie in the shade of trees which have no edible fruit, and even their inedible dates are gone. At sunset, there are gnats, and it is rough in the daytime, with sand flies biting and sucking blood from all my veins. If anyone ever opens a good jug of beer and a few come around to have a mug, two hundred big dogs and three hundred jackals, five hundred in all, appear every day on your doorstep, lured by the smell of the beer as soon as the jug is opened."

The heat is unbearable, his Egyptian comrades are sick—one has spasms, another has a toothache and an inflammation of his face—and his only comfort in despair is a small, tame jackal.

The soldier's lot was hard. He was called up for service in the Asian provinces and marched off to the border fortresses. There his trials began.

During the long desert marches he drinks water only every third day, and it smells bad and tastes of salt. He gets diarrhea, the enemy descends upon him and surrounds him with flying arrows, and he loses all hope of survival. They call to him, "Forward, brave warrior, and earn yourself a famous name!" But by now he is almost unconscious with fright. Things are no better when, to his amazement, the victory is won and the prisoners are to be led home to Egypt. A captured woman, who has fainted from fatigue on the march, is loaded on the poor soldier's back. Then, when he drops his bag of provisions, he can't pick it up, burdened as he is, and others take it from him. If he manages to survive, contrary to all expectations, he returns home a wreck, ruined by all the marches. If he deserts, his whole family is put in prison.

So might life present itself to the common man in the time between the 1500s and the 1000s, which was Egypt's age of glory, when Egyptians held complete sway over the Sinai region and all Palestine.

Then followed a period of political weakness, when foreign conquerors succeeded each other on the throne—first Libyans, then Ethiopians. Initially, there was no great power in the Middle East which could threaten the eastern border, but the powerful Assyrian kingdom emerged and conquered Palestine. The vital city of Gaza, the gate of invasion of Egypt, fell into Assyrian hands, and the consequences were the usual ones. The Assyrians seized not only the Delta, but managed to drive all the way to Thebes in Upper Egypt, the legendary capital of the earth, whose fall and plundering shocked the contemporary world. An echo is heard in the prophecy of Nahum against Assur:

"Art thou better than populous No [Thebes], that was situate among the rivers? . . . Yet was she carried away, she went into captivity: her young children also were dashed in pieces at the top of all the streets: and they cast lots for her honourable men, and all her great men were bound in chains."

For Egypt, the Assyrian invasion was not of great consequence, for the Assyrian kingdom soon went under and the Egyptians were again able to free themselves. The Pharaohs now tried at all costs to gain control over Palestine, in competition with the Babylonians, and one of them, the Pharaoh Neko, succeeded in conquering all Palestine and Syria for a brief time. But the tide of war turned, and in the year 605 the Babylonians were able to drive the Egyptians from the Asian provinces and capture Gaza as well. This time Egypt escaped occupation because of political developments within Babylonia, which prevented the Babylonians from pursuing the attack, despite their advantage.

After a time of relative peace on the northeastern border, came the fatal blow. The Persians had conquered the whole Babylonian realm and now they attacked Egypt. In the year 525 the Egyptian forces were crushed near the city of Pelusium in the east Delta, and the Persians occupied the entire country. On the battlefield, which he visited about one hundred years later, the Greek historian Herodotus made some rather curious anthropological experiments:

"There I saw something quite remarkable, about which I questioned the natives. The bones of those who had fallen in this battle had been put in separate places, so that the Persians' bones lay in one lot, and the Egyptians' in another.

"The skulls of the Persians are so fragile that if you only tap them with a pebble, you make a hole in them, while the Egyptian skulls are so hard that you can barely crack them

with a really big stone. The following reason for this is given—
and I can easily believe it—that the Egyptians shave their heads
since childhood, and therefore their skulls are hardened by
the sun."

You can just see the Greek historian, eager for knowledge, as
he makes his round of the battlefield, testing the durability
of skulls.

With minor interruptions Egypt remained a Persian province
until Alexander the Great took over the country in the year 330.
Under the Persians the lines of communications through the
Sinai desert were built up. Herodotus tells us about the pro-
vision of water on the coastal route.

"Now I want to mention something, to which few have paid
attention, when they have traveled to Egypt. From all Greece,
and from Phoenicia besides, earthen jars filled with wine are
exported to Egypt each year, and yet in all Egypt, I might
almost say that there is not a single empty wine jar. Where in
the world, you ask yourself, do they disappear to? Well, the
official in every village must collect all the earthen jars and
send them to Memphis, where they are filled with water and
sent out to the Sinai desert. In this way, all the wine jars which
come to Egypt and are emptied there, are all piled in the
Sinai desert."

The Persian king Darius also dug a canal from the eastern
arm of the Nile to the Red Sea, so that ships might pass from the
Mediterranean to the Red Sea. This was an ancestor, in other
words, of the modern Suez Canal. The reason for the great
care taken by the Persians to develop supply lines in these regions was that effective communication with Egypt was a
necessity of life for the realm. Egypt was the granary of the
Persian kingdom and the source of many other treasures as well.

With Alexander's seizure of Egypt from the Persians, there
was still no end to the eternal battles on the Sinai border. His
successors divided Alexander's great empire among themselves. The Ptolemies got Egypt, and the Seleuci got Syria,
and with that, the Sinai and Gaza once again became a bone

of contention between two great powers. Again battles raged here, with victories sometimes for the Ptolemies, sometimes for the Seleuci.

However, when Egypt became a part of the Roman Empire and the neighboring regions in Palestine and Syria were also Roman provinces, the border zone lost its great political importance for some time to come. Only toward the end of the Byzantine Empire did the battles flare up here again. The Persian King Chosroes II conquered Egypt in A.D. 619 but was driven out a few years later. At the same time, the Arabs, under Mohammed's successors, had begun their explosive expansion. The general of the first Caliph Omar, Amr Ibn el Az, defeated the Byzantines at Pelusium and within a short time took over the whole country. Egypt became a part of the great caliphate, which already in the 700s extended from Spain in the west to Persia in the east.

When Egypt became a part of this enormous realm and, thereafter, a part of the Turkish Empire, the border with Palestine, of course, assumed a minor historical role. But time and again, during the centuries that followed, right up to the present, the region became a battleground as soon as Palestine and Egypt did not belong to the same power. When Napoleon seized Egypt he also took Gaza, in the hope of being able to move from there to further conquests in the east. And in the First World War, when General Allenby moved against Turkish-held Palestine, using Egypt as his base, the major battles once again took place near Gaza.

Thus, for thousands of years wars have raged back and forth across this border zone, and soldiers have dropped from exhaustion on the desert marches along the ancient military route which links Asia and Africa. The rules of the game have always been the same. Sinai and the Gaza region have been the strategic keys. So long as the Egyptians were masters of this zone, they could effectively defend their land. If they lost control of it, Egypt's very existence was at stake.

This, then, is the history of the region, once again embattled.

Whether the old rules still hold in this time of modern mechanized armies and air power is uncertain, but history will certainly leave its imprint on the objectives and the planning of those who approach the riddle even today.

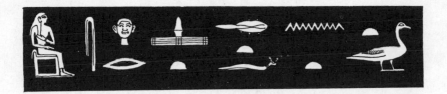

The Queen who disappeared

Few lands have presented us with as many archeological sensations as has Egypt. Large parts of the country have not as yet been thoroughly explored, and it is not so strange that remarkable new finds should still come to light. What is surprising, however, is that so many new finds should turn up in places which have first been plundered for thousands of years and then have been sifted by generations of archeologists.

To this category of archeological caches belongs the one which is perhaps best known of all, the one which every tourist customarily visits, even if he spends only a single day in Egypt. This is Giza, outside of Cairo, where the three Great Pyramids stand, built in the 2600s before Christ by the kings Cheops, Chephren, and Mycerinus.

In the burial chambers of the Great Pyramids, which have been closely examined, nothing has been found, neither mummies nor any of the fantastic treasures which must once have been placed there. The pyramids, after all, rise as great landmarks, visible for miles around, and even in their own time they must have presented a great temptation to all who were somewhat less than righteous.

So long as the pyramid builders themselves and their successors on the throne were in power, the treasures were well guarded. But we know that all the pyramids at Giza were plundered as early as the 2200s, at the end of the Old Kingdom, if not earlier. Those who later with infinite trouble broke into the burial chambers of the old kings did not find much left. And the same was true of all the tombs of courtiers around the Great Pyramids. On the whole, it is rare for any object of value to be found. The excavations are of interest primarily for architectural history.

Of all those who have worked on the graves at Giza—and there have been Germans, Austrians, Englishmen, Frenchmen, and Egyptians—only one discovered a completely undisturbed grave. This was the American Egyptologist, George Reisner.

This was not due solely to luck. More aptly, it was a reward for virtue, earned by faithful and systematic labor over a long period. He had been engaged in this work ever since 1905, excavating one part after another of the great cemetery, under the auspices of Harvard University and the Boston Museum. By 1924 he had reached the part of the necropolis which lies east of the great Cheops Pyramid. Here Reisner made an interesting discovery. When he examined the small pyramids which stand in front of the Great Pyramid, he found that the most northerly one had originally been planned to stand a little farther north. There lay a foundation which subsequently had not been used. At this stage Reisner did not understand why the move had been made. The season for excavations drew to a close, and Reisner had to return to his duties in America. His next in charge, Alan Rowe, had simply to finish off the season's work and join him later.

Then, on February 9, 1925, when Reisner's photographer had set up his camera stand to photograph a portion of the excavated burial channels, he discovered a patch of plaster on the cliff. Alan Rowe set some men working to dig out the plaster, and under it they found a hollow in the cliff which had been carefully walled off with white limestone blocks. Behind

Soldiers at a barber-
shop. From the tomb
of User-het, Thebes.
About 1430 B.C.

Metropolitan Museum of Art

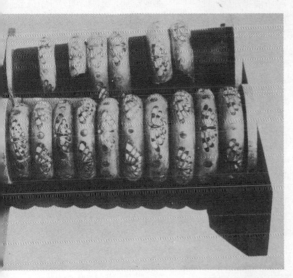

Silver armbands of
Queen Hetepheres.
From Reisner, *The
Gizeh Necropolis.*

Queen Hetepheres'
golden jewel case.
Twenty-seventh
century B.C. From
Reisner, *The Gizeh
Necropolis.*

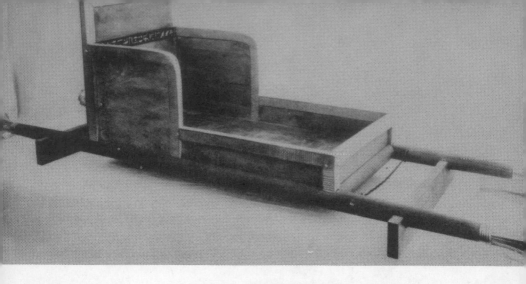

Queen Hetepheres' litter.

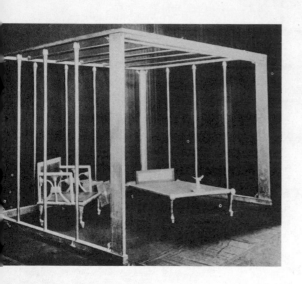

Queen Hetepheres' gilded
bedroom furniture.

The Sphinx at Giza, a symbol
of King Chefren's divinity.
Twenty-seventh century B.C.

these was a stair with twelve steps leading down into the mountain. The stairs ended in a tunnel that led horizontally to a vertical shaft that could be seen to extend both upward and downward.

They began to look around on the cliff to find the mouth of the shaft. It was not easy to locate, for the opening had been well camouflaged by the use of blocks of stone from the cliff itself. They looked around to see whether some kind of structure had not been built over the grave, as was ordinarily the case, but there was no trace of one. In short, they had chanced upon a secret grave, and they now also understood why the northernmost pyramid had been built a bit farther to the south. It was to prevent anyone working on the other pyramid from coming too close to the concealed tomb.

Now they had finally come upon something which was presumably an untouched grave from the time of Cheops, and it seemed that removing the stone barriers would go relatively quickly. They dug down farther and found one wall of stones after another, each one of which had to be carefully measured and photographed before they went on to the next. An archeological examination has to be conducted in about the same manner as a police investigation of the scene of a crime. The slightest detail must not be overlooked, since you can never know in advance exactly what problems will confront you.

In a reasonably short time, however, they got past the large stone barriers, and thereafter the shaft was filled with a mixture of stones and plaster. They descended farther and farther, expecting at any moment to find the entrance to a burial chamber. At the depth of almost thirty feet they encountered a block of stone set into the wall of the shaft. With trembling hands, they broke the block loose, tensely anticipating what might be found behind it.

But the block concealed only a small niche which contained an offering—the skull and three bones of an ox, wrapped in a rug. There were also two beer jugs, a little coal, and some chips of stone. That was all.

So they had to continue downward. The farther down they went, the more eager became the crew, which consisted of the Egyptian foreman, Said Ahmed, and four of his men. They permitted themselves no rest; the men had almost to be brought up by force when the work day was over. They dreamed of the immense riches of the royal tombs—the great find which at last was going to be made!

For Rowe, this must have been a rather terrible time. The shaft went farther and farther down, and for long stretches the walls were decayed and crumbling. The risk of rock slides was great, but Rowe felt that he could not break off the work. They reached a depth of forty-five feet, sixty feet, and still no change. The depth was completely extraordinary, and it grew increasingly difficult to work in the shaft, where the air became worse and worse, where small rocks crumbled from the walls, and where at any moment a larger rock slide might bury archeologists and workers alike under shale and stone.

But no accident occurred. Finally, at a depth of about seventy feet, they made some finds in the shaft. But these were only some earthen jars, remains of those in which the plaster had been mixed.

After twelve days of grueling work they found a wall of stone blocks like the one at the mouth of the shaft. They lifted away one block and discovered behind it a row of stones that seemed to form part of the ceiling of a burial chamber.

It was already quite late in the evening. They could not, as one usually does in Egypt, reflect down the sunlight with mirrors to get adequate illumination. Alan Rowe could light his way only with candles. Holding a candle to the opening in the wall, he looked into the crypt. He could not see exactly what was there, but he caught a glimpse of a beautiful alabaster sarcophagus. And everywhere, on the sarcophagus and on the floor of the chamber, there was the glitter of gold—gold everywhere he looked!

Not until the next morning, a month after the first trace of the grave had been found, could they get a better view. The opening was widened and the sunlight was reflected in. Then they could see the wonderful alabaster sarcophagus beside one wall. Over it lay a row of long, gilded staves, and in one spot they glimpsed an inlaid, gold platter on which they could read the name of King Snofru. Snofru was the father of Cheops, and he lay buried—this they knew—in the necropolis at Dashur, south of Giza. The whole floor was covered with pieces of gilded furniture which had fallen apart. Gold vessels could be seen, and everywhere there was a clutter of gold fragments, stone vessels, ceramics, and so forth.

Obviously, Alan Rowe felt enormous satisfaction over the fact that the long, hard work had led to such a fantastic result. But both Howard Carter (who found the treasures of Tutanchamon) and Rowe have said that the terrible responsibility struck them like a physical blow. How could they care for these treasures? They knew that what they were doing was being watched by the whole world, and that every misstep would be criticized with extreme severity, just as every step that succeeded would be taken for granted. The responsibility for dealing with such treasures so that they do not become only pieces in a puzzle which cannot be put together, is, I believe, what dominates one's thinking when one stands before such an unbelievably rich find.

Rowe felt that he could not proceed any further with the work on his own responsibility. He photographed what could be seen from the crypt opening and then had the shaft closed again. He felt that he had to turn over the rest to Reisner, the head of the whole expedition. The British military put up barbed wire, and the Cairo police and Reisner's men took over guarding the crypt.

The find was kept secret from everyone else, and the guard was effective. There was, therefore, no hurry. When Reisner finally returned to Egypt after six months, he did not try to hurry either. They knew the treasure lay well protected some eighty feet down in the cliff, and their main concern was to see that no unnecessary risks were taken. Reisner set up workrooms above the shaft, brought in an electric power line to provide light and run a fan, and even set up a primitive but effective elevator down to the crypt.

In January 1926 everything was finally clear for opening the tomb once again. Reisner rode down in the elevator and checked to make sure that all was in order. The stone block was removed, and he reassured himself that nothing had been disturbed and that no water had seeped in to damage the objects. Then they began to empty the burial chamber.

The whole operation was like a fantastic puzzle, or rather like a number of puzzles, each with many pieces all jumbled together. The puzzles now had to be reassembled. They went slowly and carefully, and only after two months of work in the chamber could they know with certainty whose tomb it was. It proved to be the grave of Cheops' mother, Hetepheres.

They kept working for 305 days, took 1057 photographs, and filled 1701 pages with sketches and notes. Thanks to this meticulous work, the various finds could be reconstructed in detail. They could begin this process on paper, but the subsequent assembly of the original pieces took several years.

Working in this manner, they were able to distinguish the objects which Queen Hetepheres had received from her consort, King Snofru. Finest of all was a set of bedroom furniture, completely covered with gold. The set included a rather short but wide bed with an inlaid footboard and a gilded headrest in place of a pillow. To the set belonged a great baldachin or canopy—you might almost call it a portable bed chamber— about ten and a half feet long, eight feet wide, and seven feet high, which was put together with boards and staves covered with gold. Some of these boards were decorated with hieroglyphics which were carved in such a way that every sign was a work of art. The whole set was precious not only because of its gold value; it was also the most beautiful furniture to have been preserved from ancient Egypt. Compared, for example, to Tutanchamon's furniture, approximately 1300 years younger, it stands on a completely different level in terms of taste.

From her son, King Cheops, who buried her, Queen Hetepheres had received, among other things, a jewel chest, a simple square case covered with gold. Inside it lay the things which were most precious in their time—namely, silver arm bracelets with inlaid butterflies in turquoise, lapis lazuli, and carnelian. Furthermore, she had with her her make-up case, manicure implements, knives—there were razors for shaving, too—a gold sewing needle, some gold vessels, and a number of other precious objects.

Because Reisner had taken such infinite pains to note all the circumstances of the find, he was indeed faced with the task of a policeman at the scene of a crime. He found, in short, that the effects in the burial chamber had not originally been placed in the tomb at Giza. All of them had been packed in cases and brought here from another grave.

Reisner, who knew very well the order in which objects were usually placed in a grave, could see that the order in which these had been arranged was the reverse of the usual. Furthermore, he found among the effects in the grave some fragments which could not be explained except by the conclusion that the original grave in Dashur, where the queen had certainly been buried at the side of her consort, King Snofru, had been plundered by thieves. For example, there were some stones with mortar on them which formed a grave entrance when fitted together. These stones, then, were part of the entrance to the tomb which the thieves had broken through in Dashur.

Now it was clear that this grave at Giza had been hidden to prevent anyone from once again disturbing the queen's eternal rest.

After 305 days of extremely taxing labor, the strain proved too great for Reisner. He became ill, and the last stage of the work, the opening of the sarcophagus, was postponed. A couple of months passed before the work was resumed, but at last the formal opening of the sarcophagus was to take place, in the presence of the minister of public works and a representative of the Boston Museum. The United States minister to Egypt was also present.

This was a unique occasion, for they now expected to view the first mummy from the time of Cheops. No one knew how mummies from this era looked or how they were adorned. Now at last they would find out.

They made sure that the seals placed on the cover of the sarcophagus when the work was done had not been broken before. Then jacks were placed under the lid of the coffin, and the lid was slowly raised. It took ten minutes to raise it high enough for them to look inside and find—that it was completely empty. All of them stood there with long faces, and Reisner brooded over how this could have happened. The most important thing in the grave was the body, but the body was gone. After all, farther up in the shaft, they had even found remains of offerings which Cheops must certainly have made to the body of the dead queen.

Thanks once again to his meticulous analyses, Reisner could reconstruct the events behind the curious fact that an empty sarcophagus stood right in the midst of this unbelievable store of furniture and treasures placed there solely for the eternal well-being of this mummy. Reconstructing the events, he concluded that when the Great Pyramids were being built at Giza, all attention was concentrated there. Down in Dashur, where the father, King Snofru, and his wife Hetepheres were buried, there were only a few burial priests and workers in the necropolis. There they were left more or less to themselves, and they knew that in the grave of the queen lay unbelievable treasures. The temptation grew too strong, and one night someone seized the opportunity and broke into the crpyt. The furniture and other objects were too difficult to carry off. Everyone knew that the real treasures were on the mummy itself, inside the alabaster coffin.

They must hurry; the guard may come at any moment. The cover of the sarcophagus is pried open with copper wedges, the mummy is removed and carried out through the shaft. In some hidden place the mummy wrappings are unwound with feverish haste, and the body is dismembered to free bracelets, necklaces, and costly belts. Now the queen's abused body lies scattered among the graves, this body on which so much pious love had been expended to ensure its preservation for eternity. When the thieves disappear, the jackals of the cemetery come forth. Queen Hetepheres' earthly remains no longer exist.

Perhaps the very next day the crime is discovered. It is reported to the vizier, the king's most trusted servitor. He travels immediately to Dashur, knowing that mortal danger awaits him should the king learn what has happened. If it becomes known that the mummy has disappeared, probably he and all the others responsible for the security of the realm will be executed. The vizier makes an investigation. He and his closest confidant replace the lid of the sarcophagus, so that the worst of the crime—the theft of the mummy—is concealed. Then he returns to Cheops and presents a carefully doctored report.

In the most soothing tones he tells the king that his mother's tomb has been disturbed by men of ill will. However, thanks to the watchfulness of His Majesty's servants, no great harm has been done. Nevertheless, perhaps it might be safer to move the body and its burial accoutrements to Giza, the royal necropolis, where they can be more effectively guarded.

The king allows himself to be deceived. Everything is removed from the grave at Dashur, emptying it completely so that no trace remains of what has actually taken place. All of the contents are put in cases, and with the sarcophagus borne first and all the treasures carried in cases behind it, everything seems quite in order. With his mind at ease, Cheops permits the grave shaft to be filled in and makes an offering to his dead mother. But he is aware now of the danger, and he does everything to conceal this second grave at Giza. The mouth of the grave shaft is camouflaged, and no one engaged in the constructions at Giza is allowed to go near the grave. The workers who prepare Hetepheres' last resting place are, no doubt, silenced forever. Only the king, the vizier, and his confidant know the location of the queen's grave.

The secret which the vizier hid from King Cheops did not come to light until it was revealed by the detective work of the American Egyptologist Reisner 4500 years later.

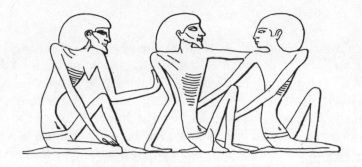

The time of revolution

Up on the sun-baked desert plateau, just where the Nile begins to widen across the great flat stretches of the Delta, there
is a swarm of people. Like a mountain rises the Great Pyramid
built by King Chephren's father, Cheops. It is 480 feet high,
as high as ten modern three-story houses piled on top of each
other, and over 2,300,000 blocks of stone had to be brought
here in order to finish it. The smooth exterior is polished to a
high gloss, and the smooth, light yellow limestone blinds the
onlooker. During the entire time of the king's rule thousands
of men have worn themselves out in building this colossus,
which now stands ready in all its glory.

Around the pyramid clusters a whole city of square tombs.
Here lie all the great men of the realm, buried like a guard and
an attentive court around their master.

If one were to think of what the Cheops Pyramid, the temples, and the noble graves which belonged to it, actually cost
the country, it would seem that its resources should have been
exhausted for some time to come. But now the new king,

Chephren, is engaged in building another equally enormous structure.

It is now the height of the building season here. The Nile has overflowed its banks, and cultivation of the soil is suspended. They will wait until the water has receded again, and the rich mull which the Nile leaves behind after each overflowing can be plowed into the soil. By the tens of thousands, workers and peasants stream to the scene of Chephren's great pyramid construction. Boatload after boatload arrives with white limestone blocks from the stone quarries on the opposite shore, and swarms of workers move the blocks over onto wooden sledges. Then the workers are hitched up to the sledges like oxen, and under the cracks of the foremen's whips, they pull the burden up brick ramps to the dizzy heights of the pyramid.

Now and then boats arrive with still longer journeys behind them. Over six hundred miles farther up the Nile Valley the Nile courses in wild torrents through a granite barrier, and there other troops of workers are toiling. In the stone quarries they are carving out gigantic granite pillars and roofing beams that weigh up to three hundred tons. These will be used in the temple at the base of the pyramid, where, every day throughout eternity, the priests will present offerings to the king's statues.

Still farther south, in the blazing heat of the Nubian deserts, Egyptian patrols are roving about in search of other kinds of stone. They have just discovered a really beautiful and rare variety. Of course, it is all of thirty-five miles from the river, and there is very little water on the way. But what does it matter? There are plenty of people, and the "miserable" Nubians can help draw the stone and build boats up in Nubia. Through the rapids farther north, a navigable channel has been cut with infinite trouble, so that it will not be necessary to reload along the way.

How can this land be constituted, with king after king expending endless labor on something like a pyramid, and to

"The skies are clouded over . . ."
Pyramid of Chephren, Giza. Twenty-seventh century B.C.

The court dwarf, Seneb, and his family. Twenty-third century B.C. Kunstgeschichtliches Seminar, Marburg.

what purpose? How can King Chephren get all of these people to wear themselves out on something so impractical and unprofitable for the land as a royal tomb and temple? And most of them even do it willingly.

The land is rich and powerful, the only really great realm in the world of its time. Far off in Babylon a number of small kingdoms are still warring with each other, unable to combine into a major state. No nation dares attack Egypt; instead, all her neighbors send gifts to keep peace with Pharaoh. The country is well organized. All grain is delivered to the king's storehouses, and in bad years there are always reserves to be tapped. True, no one has full rights of ownership over anything, but this is not necessary either, since the king looks after everyone.

To live in this way, like unreasoning cattle, with one man alone owning all and deciding all, would seem unbearable to us, no matter how prosperous or well organized the state. But we do not have the same religious faith as the Egyptians who slaved for Pharaoh.

They do not believe that they are working for an ordinary mortal. Generation after generation has been raised in the faith that the king is the greatest of all the nation's gods, the eldest god, who maintains life in all things. If he does not will it, the Nile will not overflow, and there will be crop failures and famine in Egypt. It is only thanks to him that one can live at all. If he did not exist, one would simply disintegrate after death, instead of having, as now, a fine grave in which to live for eternity, eating and drinking to the end of time.

Yet it must be obvious to everyone that even the king himself dies; after all, it is his grave which they are building. "No," is the answer. "The king does not die." When he dies, as we say, he rises into the heavens and there he rules over all the gods. All pious Egyptians labor for the king as though it were a sacrament, and all think with emotion of the day when the hymn of his ascension will sound in the great pillared halls of the pyramid's temple.

The skies cloud over, the stars are obscured,
The vaults of heaven shake, the limbs of the earth-god
   tremble,
All is still.
When they behold the king in all his divine power,
The dwellers of heaven serve him.
He roves across the heavens,
He roams through every land,
He, the most powerful, who has might over the mighty,
He, the great one, is like a falcon who soars above all
   falcons.
A god is he, older than the eldest.
Thousands serve him, hundreds make offerings to him.
His lifespan is eternity,
The borders of his power are infinity.

Some generations later the picture looks entirely different. Now reigns a king named Pepi II. Six years old when he ascended the throne, he would reach a hundred before he died. No king in the history of the world has ever reigned so long. But his rule was not so fortunate as it was long. The pyramids are like measures of royal power and the nation's wealth, and Pepi II's Pyramid doesn't look very impressive in comparison with Cheops' and Chephren's giant structures.

In Pepi II's Pyramid temple there are beautiful reliefs which picture the king's life, and the whole effect is rather imposing. We see, for instance, how he takes the field with his army against the peoples of the Libyan desert and returns in triumph with the Libyan prince and his family as captives. But we should not let appearances deceive us into believing that Pepi was a great warrior. All the reliefs are only copies of depictions of the wars of earlier kings, and if we read the names of the Libyan prince and his family, we find that no one has even bothered to make up new ones. They are precisely the same Libyans who had apparently been put to death or taken to Egypt as captives by an ancestor of Pepi II long before. It is just as though the present king of Sweden were to set up reliefs depicting his victories over Czar Peter of Russia, and we can suspect with good reason that there was not much to King Pepi's triumph over the Libyans.

A number of Pepi II's courtiers lie buried in the vicinity of the pyramid, but there are no longer so many. The royal dwarf, Seneb, custodian of the king's wardrobe, was given a fine grave here. King Pepi must have been very fond of him, for he gave him one of his own daughters in marriage. To marry off a princess to a royal dwarf would have been unheard of in Chepren's time, when the royal power was still strong, for it would have meant pollution of the king's divine blood.

Pepi's prestige has received several blows, and there are many in the land who no longer accord much authority to his commands.

How did it happen that the king has so completely lost his standing as the land's highest god, on whom the weal and woe of God and man alike depended?

Even those kings who followed Chephren had had to limit their pyramids to significantly smaller structures, and each of them raised a temple at least as costly as his own to the sun god Re in Heliopolis. Now the king is no longer portrayed as being enthroned in solitary majesty. Other gods stand as equals by his side in sculpture, and the king is always portrayed in postures of filial respect toward the sun god, who has now assumed the king's place at the head of the divine troop.

In the burial texts there is no longer anyone who trembles when the king ascends to heaven. In fact, in order to approach his father Re, he must show proof of legitimacy, a passport, and the pass comptroller is the boatman of the ferry which will transport the king to the heavenly abodes. Even this minor official in the divine hierarchy subjects the king to a thorough inquisition, and the king must beg politely for permission to proceed in order to entertain the gods as a dancing dwarf, to serve as an oarsman in the sun ship, or best of all, to be the sun god's secretary. In all things, the king is answerable to his father Re and must make a full accounting to him. One text says of the king: "There is no evil which he has done. This is a statement which has great importance before Thy visage, oh Re!"

Perhaps it was the essential religious force of the sun worship which converted the king and made him step down from his place as the supreme god. Perhaps this, too, impelled him to load the priests of this god with riches and lands, so that they might tend the daily offerings to Re. Who can tell what took place in the heart of the divine ruler? Once done, it could not be undone. The religious and economic power which the priests had once been given was difficult to take back again.

There were probably many who did not understand how this had occurred, and who wished it had never happened. For their edification, an account of the supposed events had been circulated already in the time of Cheops.

One day King Cheops was bored and sought to amuse himself by watching various magicians practice their arts. His mood, not very cheery to begin with, grew worse when one of the magicians, who had been directed to fetch a mystical implement from a temple, declared quite unexpectedly: "I am not he who can bring it, but the eldest of the children whom Rededet now bears [shall do so.]" In answer to the king's question, he explains: "Rededet is the wife of a priest of the sun god Re and she is pregnant with three male children, whose father is the god Re. He has promised her that they shall exercise royal power in this land."

In other kings, Cheops' dynasty would be cast out and replaced by other kings, children of the sun god Re. Cheops tried to prevent the children's birth, but he failed to do so because of intervention by the gods, and the prophecy of the magician was fulfilled.

If this was indeed the way in which the royal dynasty which succeeded Cheops' family attained power, it was only proper that the rulers should show filial devotion and gratitude to their divine father Re. When this family was in turn succeeded by the dynasty to which Pepi II belonged, other consequences of the reduction in royal divinity and authority became apparent.

The provincial governors, who were formerly dependent on the king and who were transferred from one province to the other lest they become too firmly entrenched in a single district, now made themselves increasingly independent. Their offices became hereditary, and they ruled and disposed as they pleased in their provinces, even if they outwardly affected a proper subservience. In order to manage the increasingly dissolute governors, particularly in upper Egypt, Pepi appointed a trusted aide as "Chief of the Upper Egyptian Governors." The first man who had this task may have done some good, but the whole plan soon degenerated. "Chief of the Upper Egyptian Governors" became an empty honorary title, which one governor after another assumed or received as a reward.

Revenues flow into the state treasury ever more sluggishly Pepi II comes to be ruler of the country in name only. And so the power in the realm becomes more and more diffused; increasing numbers want to share the exercise of authority, and the situation grows worse and worse.

Finally, the whole structure collapses. The soldiers of the legions begin to plunder instead of defending the country's borders. Asian and Libyan hordes invade the land in the north. Everything begins to topple.

Then even the broad popular stratum rises against the king, and a terrifying revolution stalks the land.

The costly statues in the temples of the pyramids are overturned and broken. The holy pictures of the gods, in gold, are stolen or hidden away by the priests. Everywhere plundering bands roam the countryside. Nothing is holy to them; everything is pulled down into dreadful chaos.

Across thousands of years the voice of this time still speaks to us and depicts the horrors of the age.

"We do not know what has happened in the land. The poor now have riches; he who before could not afford sandals is now a rich man.

"Everyone thinks only of violence. Pestilence ravages the land. Blood flows everywhere. Masses of corpses are thrown into the river. The river has become the usual burial place.

"The nobles sorrow, but the poor people rejoice.

"In all cities, they say, 'Let us persecute the great men among us.' Look, people walk about like filthy birds of prey. Vermin overrun the country, no one wears white clothes nowadays.

"The land whirls about like a potter's wheel.

"Behold, the river is full of blood. When you seek to drink from it, you recoil, for after all it is water that you thirst for. The crocodiles in the river are sated with the dead they have to eat. Willingly people cast themselves to them. Evil times have fallen upon the land.

"Behold, the desert is encroaching on the land. The provinces are being ravaged. Foreign hordes are descending on Egypt's land. There is no longer room for the Egyptians themselves.

"Now gold and lapis lazuli, silver and malachite, carnelian and precious jewels hang about the necks of slave girls. But distinguished ladies go dressed in rags. Mothers of households sigh: 'If we only had something to eat!'

"Behold, the children of princes are crushed against the wall. There is no food, the princes starve in misery. But the servants are well supplied. One eats only vegetables and washes them down with water. One takes food from the mouths of swine.

"No one rejoices any longer. Sorrow stalks the land, followed by lamentation and wails of woe.

"High and low alike say: 'If only I might die!'

"Small children cry: 'Would that I had never been born!'

"All warehouses are plundered and the guards are slaughtered. They have broken into the state offices and carried off the tax rolls. The bondsmen make themselves lords and have slaves themselves. The records of those who keep account of the corn are destroyed. Egypt's grain becomes the property of every man.

"The legal texts from the courts of justice are cast into the front hall. Men trample them in the streets. The populace rips them to shreds in the alleys.

"Behold, the flame leaps high! Now happens that which has never happened before. The king is dragged away by the populace, he who was buried as a god. That which the pyramid concealed is gone. A handful of lawless men have dared to deprive the land of its king. Behold, they have dared to challenge the king's divine power. In the work of one moment, the regime has been felled. The inhabitants of the palace are gripped with fear.

"Behold, so it has come to pass: the poor in the land have become rich, and the rich have been wiped out. Officials are driven from place to place. The country's leaders flee the land. The corps of officials is like a frightened herd of sheep without a shepherd.

"The land weeps.

"Everything lies in ruins!"

Thus the first great state in the history of the world is shattered. Material well-being in the land is gone, famine rages, and no one's life is safe.

This is not only a material bankruptcy. All spiritual values have been lost as well. There are no longer any accepted norms. Instead, every man must stand on his own legs and find himself an ideal. The Egyptians are forced to become individualists, a terrifying experience for a people who have been the most pronounced collectivists imaginable.

In all texts from this time after the revolution, we find a typical postwar mentality, a fumbling and searching for a faith to live by in a night of despair. Various ideals and various solutions to life's questions are tested, but we can always hear some of the inner nagging doubt in these voices which reach us after the thousands of years which have passed.

In the king's divinity and his sheltering might, one can no longer believe. He has become only a weak mortal who cannot even protect himself.

And the gods seem to have abandoned Egypt, since the situation is so desperate. What can one then rely upon?

One faith most of them had left, faith in a life after this one. How things would be after death was really the most important question. Here on earth one would have to try and survive in one way or another. This was, after all, something temporary, but the life after death lasted for eternity.

Faith in a life after this one is now no longer only something inspirational, as it had been before. Now one is afraid that conditions may be as bad in the realm of the dead as it was on earth. Perhaps a thousands dangers threaten one there also.

Anxiety about death begins to take hold everywhere.

Many put their faith in sorcery and magic. If you can only rely on what these promise, all difficulties are dissolved. You have only to wish for something and utter the proper formulas while performing the proper magical rites, and the wishes are fulfilled, giving you power over all things. Then, of course, you might turn yourself into a dangerous beast of prey which could tear your enemies to bits. Like a falcon, you could fly high in the sky, locate your enemy, swoop down upon him, and rip him apart. What you lacked the power to do in this world, where enemies kill your relatives and steal everything you own, you should surely be able to do in the world of the dead.

If one knew the right formulas, one might even acquire power over the gods and force them to return the dead family mourned here on earth. And one might descend into the underworld as a feared and respected man.

"Behold, I descend into the kingdom of death to embrace my family. If I am not immediately given back my father, my mother, and all that are mine, I shall see to it that the sun god can no longer ascend his heavenly ladder. Meat shall no longer be offered on the altars of the gods; no bread shall be broken for them; animals shall no longer be slaughtered for them. On the execution block of the sun god, I shall chop off the heads of every soul and every god who deprives me of my family!

"Behold, rejoicing I descend, for my family has been restored to me. Rejoicing, the eldest of my family comes forward to meet me as I approach. They cast their tools to the ground, for I have freed them from working for others any longer."

To stand alone in the unknown world, abandoned by friends and relatives, was the most terrible prospect imaginable. Never before had one felt so dependent upon them as now in this hopeless anarchy. But if the family became impoverished or if all died, who would then ensure that the dead were supplied with food in their graves? If they were not, they would have to go hungry throughout eternity, reduced to begging their way. Here again magic might help. If one could not depend on others to attend to one's needs, one would have to take along attendants in the grave.

The graves are now filled with small wooden models representing servants threshing and grinding and baking bread, slaughtering and cooking. Others are weaving or brewing beer. A few boats are also taken along. Since one must have a boat to travel in Egypt, it may be a necessity in the realm of the dead as well. Thus one hopes to avoid faring badly in the next world. Thanks to the small wooden figures, one might even fare well. If there are wars in the next world as in this one, maybe armies of toy soldiers, placed in the grave, can help to bring victory over enemies.

And so, many people build dream castles about how grand everything will be after death. Then it is only natural that they also long for escape from hard reality to this dream world beyond the grave.

> Death stands before me today
> like health returning to the sick,
> like rising up from the sickbed.

> Death stands before me today
> like the scent of myrrh,
> like sitting beneath a sail with the wind blowing.

Death stands before me today
like the scent of lotus blossoms,
like sitting on the shores of drunkenness.

Death stands before me today
like the departure of a storm,
like returning home from the wars.

Death stands before me today
like a clearing in the sky.

. . . . .

Death stands before me today
like the longing for home,
after many years as a captive.

So speaks, in a text from this time, a man tired of life, ad-
dressing his soul and trying to lure it with him to the other
world. But the soul wants him to live on in this world and
tears down his dream of a happy life after this one. No doubt
it is sensible to use all the means of religion and magic to plan
as well as possible for the life after death. Perhaps a ritual
burial, a well-equipped grave, and daily sacrifies to the dead
really will do some good. Perhaps not. Who knows? But one
ought not to be so foolish as willingly to give up the known
for the unknown, to exchange life with all its richness and its
joys for the uncertainties death may bring. It is better to take
each day as it comes. "Eat, drink, and be merry—tomorrow
you will die!" is the basic content of the soul's answer.

This skepticism toward religion and magic, this reaction
against exaggerated pessimism also finds expression in a song
written in the time when the old values had gone under. With
some variations this song was sung for centuries thereafter by
the blind bards, who played their harps at festive banquets.

Thoughts of burial
bring forth tears and make men melancholy.

G. Eriksson

Voyage into the unknown. Model boat from the Time of the Revolutions, twenty-second century B.C. Victoria Museum, Uppsala.

"Death stands before me today." Statue from the Time of the Revolutions, twenty-second century B.C. In the background, battle pictures from Deshashe, twenty-fourth century B.C.

G. Eriksson

"Make every day a festival." The blind harpist sings the song of life and death. Relief from the fourteenth century B.C. Leyden Museum.

The solitary one, Sesostris III. Nineteenth century B.C.
From *L'Encyclopedie Photographique de l'Art*.

For this means dragging a man from his home
and casting him out on the bare mountain.
Never can he rise from his grave
to look at the sun.

All those who built themselves graves of granite,
as soon as they died, their altars stood bare,
just like those who tired and died on the bank of the river
without family.

I have heard the speeches of wise men,
whose words still live on our lips.
Where are their dwellings now?
Their burial monuments no longer exist,
as though they had never been.

No one comes back from the land hence,
to tell us how they fare,
to tell us what they need,
to comfort our hearts,
until we are also there
where they went.

Therefore enjoy yourself
and let your heart forget
that someday—in the grave—
you will be made blissful!
Do what you want, so long as you live.
Put myrrh on your head,
Dress yourself in the finest linen,
and anoint yourself with the balm of the gods.

Make of every day a feast
and do not tire.
Look, you can't take with you what you own.
Look, no one who has gone away has ever returned.

Despite all the injustice here on earth, which can cause one to doubt everything, some ideas still live on from the shattered concept of the just society. Perhaps after all there is a divine justice. Perhaps the god of the underworld sits in judgment upon the dead. Not everyone believes entirely in this divine tribunal, but if it should be true and if one were judged according to one's actions, well, then there is only one salvation—a righteous life.

"Do that which is right, so long as you live on earth. Comfort the weeping, deal gently with a widow. Deprive no man of the goods inherited from his fathers and take not from the great men their property. Punish no one unjustly. Kill no one.

"The man who is gentle shall enjoy a happy life.

"You know that the judges in the kingdom of death will not be gentle on that day when the wretched are judged. Do not rely on the length of the years which remain to you, for to the gods an entire lifetime in like an hour.

"Only man lives on after death, and his deeds are piled in a stack before him. He remains in the realm of death for an eternity, and a fool is he who believes this is [easily] endured.

"But he who arrives there without having sinned shall be like a god there."

It is a king who says this. His name is Merikare, and he reigns in Heracleopolis in northern Egypt.

His father had begun his rule with great success, wreaking havoc among the foreign trespassers on the Delta in the north. When the provincial princes in southern Egypt were no longer willing to pay taxes to him, he began a war against them. His luck held, and he conquered city after city.

But then came a battle by the holy city of Thinis, where the land's first kings lay buried. A terrible sacrilege was committed —the holy graves were plundered during the heat of the battle. This put wind in the sails of the enemy. Surely a king responsible for such outrages could not be he who would bring justice and order to the land. Increasing numbers go over to the side of the provincial rulers, and they move northward victoriously. Powerless, Merikare, who has now succeeded his father, can only look on as they plunder his father's grave in retribution.

In this desperate position, Merikare tries to influence wavering minds with propaganda. He issues a tract in which he has his father speak to his son and give him advice on ruling. A masterly trick! In this way Merikare could criticize and disavow his father's policies without seeming to be disrespectful and lacking in piety.

Granted, the father had taken a harsh course, the sacred had been profaned, and terrible events had transpired, but now things would be better. No doubt "battles will never cease in Egypt," he writes; it would be purely utopian to promise to establish eternal peace in this age of confusion. But those who align themselves on his side shall be richly rewarded. The great will retain their riches, and the poor will be protected. The king will punish neither too strictly nor unjustly. Only he who promotes insurrection need fear the penalty of death, and even he may be spared if he is related to the king or is a childhood friend.

It is not only in the afterlife that man is delivered over to the judgment of the gods, to whom he must answer for his deeds. Here on earth as well, all is in the hands of the gods.

"Generation after generation passes. God, who knows the changing conditions, has remained hidden. No one can fend off the blow of the lord's hand." Therefore one must keep in the god's favor through rich offerings, but still more important, through righteousness, "for the virtue of the righteous man is preferred to the sinner's ox."

There is still another thing which all should consider—most particularly, of course, the opponents of Merikare. The standing of royal prestige and the judgment of posterity should persuade the enemy not to deal harshly with a king, a colleague.

"To wield royal power is a glorious office, for even if there is no son or brother to tend his memorials, one king will still do another a good turn. One man does something for his predecessor, so that what he has done may be done for him by his successor."

This was a thought which was phrased long after: "Do unto others as you would have them do unto you."

For one who was in danger of being made to answer for his deeds, right here and now, by his royal competitors and enemies, it was only natural to preach mercy as a royal virtue and to underscore strongly that even a king was responsible to the gods for his conduct. It was worth noting, too, that good fortune and success were ephemeral things, that power and wealth in this world were far less important than being able to bear up well under divine examination at the judgment of the dead, when virtue was rewarded and sin earned eternal punishment.

But this confession of sins, the promises of better things, even these ideals which properly applied might perhaps have given men a firm faith, inner peace, and a sense of purpose in life, were of no avail to Merikare.

His peace efforts failed, and the civil war raged on. The rulers of Thebes, who had now raised themselves to be kings, crushed all opposition, united the country into one realm, and their might went unchallenged for half a century.

But the era of misfortunes was not yet past. Once again the land would be plunged into anarchy. The vizier of the Theban kings seized power for himself. In some way he had to justify this usurpation, for enough order had been established in the meantime so that it was no longer self-evident that whosoever might be stronger could topple the ruling house.

The vizier's name was Amenemhet, more commonly called Ameni. He, too, resorted to a propaganda tract to show how necessary it was to replace the old royal house with new blood. The simplest way was to depict in shocked tones the sad state of the nation, a method we recognize all too well. If one can only make people really conscious of their dissatisfactions, much has been done to set the stage for a change of government.

The nation's sorrows are portrayed in the most vivid colors. While much of this picture may be true, the propaganda does its best to make it seem still worse. The Asians have crossed the borders, we are told, and Egyptians slaughter each other.

The weight of taxation is unbearable. "The land lies wasted, but the taxes demanded are great. The grain is scanty, but the bushels in which the grain tax is measured out are large and filled to overflowing." Moreover, there are several rivals for power and each one exacts his own tax. "The country has become small, but its rulers [have become] numerous."

Even the gods and the forces of nature have abandoned the land. The sun does not shine as it should and the Nile is drying up. Everything is upside down. The misery is so great that no one has any tears left.

The only salvation is to get a new ruler, to place a god on the throne again, as in the time when the pyramids were built, a time to which all look back as the happiest and richest in Egypt's history.

Then the propaganda text rings out in prophetic words that a savior shall come in this time of need. The savior, of course, is the one who composed the prophecy to convince everyone that it was necessary that he and he alone be king.

Watch, a king shall come from the south, Ameni is his name.
He shall wear the country's crown and place the diadem on his head.
In his time, men will rejoice.
All those who are ill-willed shall close their mouths for fear of him.
The Asians will be mowed down by him, and the Libyans will fall before his fire.
A wall will be built on the border and the Asians will no longer be allowed to break into Egypt. They shall once again beg water for their cattle as was their fate in the past.
Justice will once again be honored and injustice hunted down. He shall rejoice who may see this and then serve the king.

And so, this Ameni-Amenemhet becomes absolute ruler of the land. The old traditions from the time of the pyramids are to be resurrected. The king shall be like a god, infallible and exalted over everything and all. But much had happened since the days of King Chephren, when all were inspired with faith and love for the king and believed that he was the supreme god. What had taken place in the meantime could not be dismissed as though it had never occurred. The king himself could no longer feel safe and secure. He remembered that he himself seized power by force and how many there were who had ascended the throne by the same means, only to be cast down one day.

The king who would be a god has become a bitter and hardened man. Bitter also is his advice to his son on how he should rule in the land. Force, not right or the people's trust, is the key to power in this post-revolutionary time.

"Mount the throne like a god. Be king of the land and rule over its shores.

"Take care with your subjects! Never approach them alone!

"Don't rely on a brother! Have no friend! Permit yourself no confidants! It gains you nothing.

"When you sleep, see to your own safety, for on the day one's luck runs out, one has no followers."

These words read like a reply to Merikare's political tract, and this text, too, was a piece of propaganda, employed by the ruler in a dangerous situation. Amenemhet was already dead when it was written, and it was his son, Sesostris I, who circulated the tract to justify himself to his own time and to posterity.

Amenemhet had fallen victim to a harem intrigue, and in Sesostris' propaganda text, Amenemhet tells his own story of the events:

"I gave to the poor and raised up the humble. I granted audiences to those who were nothing, as well as those who were important.

"But he who ate my bread committed treason against me. He to whom I gave my hand plotted against me. He who dressed in my fine linen regarded me as a shadow, and they who anointed themselves with my myrrh treated me as though I were dead. My pictures and my necklaces had been distributed [as remembrances] among these people, but they would remember me in a way of which one has never heard mention before, and they would let me wage a fight which no one has ever seen before. When the fight came, the yesterdays were forgotten.

"It does not pay to do good to him who forgets one whom he should remember.

"It was after the evening meal and night had fallen. I allowed myself a few moments of rest and lay down on my bed. I was tired and my thoughts longed for peace.

"But then weapons were being distributed. The chief of my bodyguards defended me, but the others were like snakes in the desert. I was awakened by the struggle, I alone. I found a man dead. It was the chief of the guard. If I had immediately taken up arms, I could have driven off the cowardly wretches with a lance. But no one is strong at night, and one cannot succeed without help.

"You see, the evil deed took place, when I was without you, before the court had yet heard that I was going to turn over the royal power to you, before I had had myself crowned together with you.

"Misfortune had never fallen upon me since my birth. Never had anyone been so fortunate a warrior as I."

Then follows a hymn of praise to Amenemhet's happy reign. Of course, the fact that he himself was a usurper who had seized power by force is not mentioned. In the final words comes the defense of Sesostris' measures against his adversaries:

"To be sure, many of my children are now on the street [expelled by you from the court]. He among them who is sensible, he says yes, but he who is foolish protests [against your having taken power], for because he is empty-headed, he has not understood that you, my son Sesostris, were my own tongue when I still stood on my legs, and that you were my heart, when my eyes still could see.

"Behold, I have begun it; you shall complete the work. I have landed in the realm of the dead, but you are crowned with the white crown on the son of the gods. The royal seal is now in its proper place, and in the sun boat rejoicing over you has begun.

"Ascend the throne for a regime better than mine, not for one just like mine."

Who can get a clear view of an oriental harem intrigue and distinguish the guilty from the innocent? Were Sesostris and his followers wholly without guilt, and was this propaganda simply intended to allay any suspicions that Sesostris had something to do with the murder? Or were the assassins followers of another claimant to the throne among the princes? Did Sesostris then want to underscore the fact that it really was he and no one else who had been meant to inherit the throne, and that it was his right and duty to punish his rivals, even though they were relatives? If the fact that he had driven a number of them from the court provoked anger, was this meant to appear to be a mild punishment against the background of the murder of the king?

These questions no one can answer, but men of that and later times knew that the whole truth was no more to be found in Sesostris' propaganda than in any other. But the enemies were silenced, and to posterity, this text, like the teaching of Merikare, became a classic, one of the pearls of literature, which was copied out for centuries to come so that generations growing up would learn elevated thoughts and beautiful language.

Implicit in the idea of being both a man and a god is a conflict which becomes most acute in regard to the ruler's closest contacts—brothers and sons, relatives and friends. While human instincts call for intimacy, the kingly ideal and political sense demand personal detachment. This conflict did not end with Sesostris' assumption of power.

There were still provincial lords left in the land, and they still constituted a latent threat to the king's omnipotence. Not until a century later comes the final settlement, when Sesostris III, praised in a hymn as "the divine solitary one," puts an end to the whole institution of provincial governors. There are no texts which tell us of this bitter settlement, all the more bitter because the families then expelled from the political arena were often intimately tied to the royal house by bonds of blood or friendship. Yet suddenly, with one blow, these feudal lords ceased to exist, and the details of what happened we can only imagine.

In the portraits of Sesostris III this human conflict has been expressed in a masterly way, and, as a result, it seems frighteningly real to us.

These pictures speak of human bitterness, but also of invincible energy and will to power. There we see both the divine king and the man, marked by his inner battles as well as the battles outside. The king, who was a man, but who must also be a god—the solitary one, not as a god, but as a man.

History's children of misfortune

To the average person, shards of pottery are things of no importance which belong on the trash pile. So they were also regarded in the more or less obscure eras archeologists have set themselves to study and bring to life. To the archeologists, however, the shards are important historical documents.

Then, as now, styles changed from one generation to another. Pottery, of course, was fragile and it soon got broken and had to be replaced—naturally with something up to date. The broken pieces landed on the trash pile, where they remained, in layer upon layer, with the oldest pieces on the bottom.

When archeologists unearth this kind of strata sequence, as it is called, they can follow changes in style through the years. They may also find an item or two with inscriptions—a seal,

73

for example, which indicates more or less precisely the age of the layer in which it is found. Then, by combining these results with findings from other places, they can trace somewhat more than the purely local development. Larger and larger areas of culture can be reconstructed, and one can see how ceramic wares particularly popular in one locale were spread through neighboring regions by trade or migrations of peoples. If you know the ages of the various kinds found in one place, you can use their recurrence in neighboring cultures to date the stages in which these cultures developed.

To a great extent such findings are the alpha and omega for large segments of oriental archeology. The less we can learn of the events of a period from written historical sources, the more we must reply on pure archeology, with its analyses of pottery shards and similar remnants. In regard to the earliest times, when writing had not been invented, much less historical writing, we are wholly dependent on these methods. With their help we have been able to build up quite a clear conception of at least the principal features of man's oldest cultures and their relationships to each other. But these results, often very good, have led not infrequently to a certain overestimation of what these methods can yield and the conclusions which can be drawn from the material. Misuse of a method hardly condemns the method itself, but many a good "textbook truth" can thank misapplied archeology for its existence.

Not least is this true in regard to the great migrations of peoples which are often captivating, but which just as often appear on closer study to be based solely on the fact that at a certain time a new type of ceramic ware begins to appear in one nation after another. This may very well have been due to a migration, but in many cases it is only a sign of vigorous trade.

Let us imagine that future archeologists, around the year 3000, were to study the ruins of present-day Egyptian villages, and that they had no other sources for the history of Egypt in the 1900s except the finds they made. In the layers of the first decade of the 1900s they would find quantities of storage vessels made of baked clay, ancient in style and made by a technique thousands of years old. All of a sudden, practically all of these clay vessels disappear in the layers dating from the 1930s and 1940s. Instead, there are box-shaped metal vessels. Often they bear inscriptions which after infinite pains are finally identified as American, and quite often they are decorated with a picture of a mussel shell. In short, American gasoline cans replace the older ceramic wares as water buckets and storage vessels. In the same layer they find curious appliances in place of the older hearths made of mud from the Nile, and their origin is finally traced to Sweden, though oddly enough they carry the Latin word "primus."

The archeologists predisposed to migration theories would, no doubt, formulate the following considered explanation. In the 1930s there is a new migration into Egypt, the "Gasoline-can People," probably from America, an assumption which seems all the more likely since their characteristic artifact, the gasoline can, has been found in great numbers in intermediate countries during the same era. About the same time yet another people comes to Egypt's fertile ground from the barren lands of northern Europe. Among them there may be a Latin-speaking element, since the Latin word "primus" is found on their most important artifact.

This is a caricature of a certain archeological mode of procedure, and it is hard to believe that it has been employed to any great extent. But unfortunately this is more common than one might think. In many instances you simply cannot gauge the accuracy of these theses, becauses there are no materials in the form of historical texts, for example, by which to check them. Then you have simply one view against another, and since migrations generally seem more "interesting" than trade, the more dramatic migration theory wins out, at least in the more popular presentations.

Particularly in regard to Middle Eastern history have archeological methods been often misapplied. As a prime example, one can cite the so-called "Hyksos." They were Asian conquerors who ruled over Egypt in the 1600s before Christ, during one of the more obscure periods in the nation's history. We know that they came into Egypt from Palestine, but we have very few, and, moreover, late sources to tell us anything of their origin, how they came to Egypt, and how their rule was structured during its heyday. Most of the contemporary written sources tell us only about their fate during the last period of their supremacy in Egypt. Here we have tried to fill in the gaps with the help of archeology.

First, their ethnic composition. All of their proper names, with one or two exceptions, are purely Semitic. Still some have tried to prove that among the Hyksos there were also representatives of the Hurrians, a people who then dominated the northeastern parts of what is now Syria. The only proper name which was possibly Hurrian did not prove much one way or the other; after all, not every Smith is an Englishman.

Here archeology was called in to help. In a couple of places in Egypt, in graves dating from the time of the Hyksos, some painted vases were found, vaguely reminiscent of ceramics common in the region in which Hurrian was spoken. Of course, whether there was the slightest connection between this pottery and the people who had Hurrian as their mother tongue still remained to be proved, but this did not disturb the malpractitioners of archeology, who saw in the painted vases from Egypt certain proof that among the Hyksos there were also Hurrians. The latter, in other words, were supposed to have migrated into Egypt, bringing ceramics with them from their homeland.

A closer analysis has shown that the painted vases from Egypt are of a different type from those of northern Syria. Instead, they are of a type common in Palestine, which may indeed have been influenced through a number of channels by the ceramics of the region where Hurrian was also spoken. However, a totally different ceramic ware had become dominant in this region during the time when the Hurrian-speaking elements had founded a state there. The truth was infinitely more complicated than the theory first launched. Even if the painted vases had been Hurrian artifacts, it would have proven nothing about the existence of Hurrians among the Hyksos. By that reasoning, the salons of eighteenth-century Europe would have been thronged with Chinese, considering the amount of East Indian porcelain used in them.

On similar shaky archeological ground, some have also found Aryans among the Hyksos, but let us leave this theory to its fate and examine instead the handsomest blossom among the flora of hypotheses.

With the help of archeological finds, some have thought themselves able to prove that the Hyksos once ruled a great world empire far beyond the borders of Egypt. This view is still clung to today, although the original arguments have long since lost their force. The theory emerged when a lid bearing the name of a Hyksos ruler was found in Crete, and when later a stone lion bearing the same royal name turned up in an antique shop in Bagdad. The theory would have it that the whole region from Crete in the northwest to Bagdad in the northeast had belonged to the Hyksos' sphere of political power. Such random finds really prove nothing, as most scholars soon recognized. But the great-empire theory was not dead on that account, for the pottery shards were invoked to help out.

There is one kind of ceramic ware which was regarded as such a characteristic Hyksos artifact that its occurrence in a region could be taken as proof that the Hyksos had lived there. These were small black vessels, with carved pictures, which were unearthed in various spots from Syria in the north to the Sudan in the south. For this reason, it was argued, you could still assume that the Hyksos had ruled over a very wide area. Closer analysis of the material showed that this theory was not up to the mark either, simply because we have no solid reason for attributing these vessels to the Hyksos alone. In Palestine, the land from which the Hyksos advanced into Egypt, this particular type of ceramic ware turned up even before the time of the Hyksos, the product of a long development without any break which might point to the influx of a foreign people. Furthermore, these small pots are also to be found in southern Egypt and the Sudan during a time when we know from other sources that the Hyksos had not yet reached these parts.

So, the universal empire seems more and more the product of free fantasy. As a French scholar has aptly put it, it is one of the prettiest fairy tales in Middle Eastern history.

It is, in any case, unusual that one and the same historical phenomenon should be the subject of so many sweeping speculations as have been the Hyksos rulers. One has some right to call them Egyptian history's children of misfortune.

They have not only run afoul of poor applications of archeological methods; the handling of the historical texts concerning them can also be taken as a typical example of how such sources should not be used.

From contemporary sources it is quite plain that once the Hyksos rulers had ascended Pharaoh's throne, their entire behavior was not very different from that of the domestic kings. They became completely Egyptianized, piously built temples to the nation's gods, and showed a lively interest in the old culture. As an example, we can cite the fact that our best mathematical manuscript dates from the time of the Hyksos' rule. Because of their foreign origin, however, the Hyksos became an excellent subject for later propagandists. They are used as an impressively dark background to the rule of the native Egyptian kings who succeeded them. In later times, when the land once again came under foreign rule, the Hyksos were just as useful in propaganda, proving how miserable things were when foreigners bestrode Egypt's throne. For these later independence movements, if such a modern name may be used at a time when nationalism had yet to be invented, portraying the Hyksos in the blackest terms was a nice oblique way of getting at the throats of their foreign rulers. We can plainly see, time and again, how the Hyksos are blackened more and more, until they stand forth as Huns and barbarians, blood-suckers without any culture.

The Egyptian king who began the final struggle against the foreign rulers was named Kamose, and he reigned in Thebes in upper Egypt. There, in the temple of the god Amon, he raised two memorial stones, so-called steles, on which his victorious campaign against the Hyksos is depicted. One of these, which covers the beginning of the story, has been known for some time, but only the upper part of the slab has been preserved. Fortunately some clerk amused himself by copying the inscription on a wooden tablet, so that a little more of the text was saved, but the end is still missing. The other stele, which no one knew existed, was discovered only in 1954. These texts give us quite a clear picture of the chain of events, even though many details are still uncertain.

They begin with an account of a conference in which the king and his councilors are discussing what should be done about the political situation. In northern Egypt the Hyksos rule from their capital Avaris, in the Delta. South of Elephantine, near the first cataract, the Nubians have freed themselves from the Egyptian overlordship which they have unwillingly borne for centuries, and they have established a state of their own. This situation Kamose will not tolerate:

"What good is my strength when a prince is in Avaris and another in [Nubian] Kush, and I sit [on the throne] together with an Asian and a Nubian, since each one has a piece of Egypt. One, with whom I share the land, I cannot get by to reach Memphis, which still belongs to Egypt, since he has Hermopolis [in Middle Egypt]. No man can rest under the plague of Asian taxes.

"But I shall attack him and slit open his belly. I shall save Egypt and conquer the Asians."

But the councilors said:

"Yes, the Asians' possessions extend to Kusae [in middle Egypt], but we have our portion of Egypt in peace and quiet.

[The border fortress] Elephantine is strong, and the land from there up to Kusae is ours. The best earth is plowed for us. All the way up in the Delta [in the Hyksos' region] our cattle graze, and we are sent spelt for our swine. No one raids our cattle, and no one attacks. He has the Asians' land; we have Egypt. But should someone come and attack us, we shall give him opposition.

"They displeased the heart of His Majesty," the text continues, and Kamose declares his decision to settle accounts with the Hyksos, but he does not further insist that his countrymen are being ill-treated.

From the counselors' answer to the king, it is apparent that the Hyksos at this time were not at all behaving in an intolerably demanding or power-greedy manner toward the Egyptians. Evidently one had established a *modus vivendi* acceptable to both sides. The Thebans may graze their cattle on the great pastures of the Delta, and the situation is actually advantageous for the Thebans just as it is. It would only mean an economic reverse to break openly with the Hyksos.

Against this conciliatory policy, which favors purely local interests, Kamose sets up the principle: *"Ein Volk, ein Reich, ein Führer!"*—Egypt for the Egyptians. These slogans were just as dubious then as they are in modern times, for it is doubtful whether their Egyptian brothers in the north really wished to be liberated. When the next passage tells us that the populace hailed the soldiers as liberators and greeted them with open arms, we nod again with familiarity. This type of war reporting we know all too well to take seriously.

However, a scholar would meet with skepticism if he maintained that the inscription should be interpreted in this way, considering both the facts that it was the victor who was writing the history and that the real concept of nationalism, and the ideal of independence bound up with it, were of far later date in history. Many writers on oriental history had become all too accustomed to rewriting the ancient texts in modern phrases without criticizing the sources.

Even from the first stele we learn significantly enough that the initial opponent whom Kamose defeats is an Egyptian "who had made the city of Neferusi an abode of Asians." He belonged, in other words, to those who could see no advantage to replacing Hyksos rule with a Theban military dictatorship. That the Hyksos exercised a considerably looser political control, which no doubt permitted greater freedom for the individual, is apparent simply from the fact that Kamose was able to make himself king of Thebes.

From the newly discovered stele, on which the rest of the campaign is described, it is quite clear that it was precisely the Egyptians in middle Egypt who offered hard opposition. Here Kamose forgets to picture himself as liberator and speaks frankly in an address to the Hyksos king:

"You ruin-destined Asiatic . . . you wretch, who said: 'I am master without equal all the way from Hermopolis to the upper Per-Hathor and to Avaris!'

"I, Kamose, left this region laid waste and uninhabited. I destroyed its cities and burned its dwellings, so that they would be scorched mounds for eternity [as punishment] for the harm they have done to Egypt, when they set themselves to serve the Asians, after having abandoned Egypt, their mistress, in her troubles."

Thus, according to the account, the aggression was directed more against compatriots than against the Hyksos. A find from the grave of Amenophis I, a king who died a half century after Kamose, indicates that hatred of the Hyksos had not yet developed by this time. This was an alabaster vase bearing the name of a Hyksos king. Since the Egyptians customarily obliterated the names of enemies so that they would not live on, the men of Amenophis' time must have had a more favorable, objective view of the Hyksos than became the case later.

The real hate propaganda first appears three generations after the Asian rulers had been driven out of Egypt. So far as we can see, it was Queen Hatshepsut who launched it. As a woman on the throne, she needed all the support propaganda could supply. In one text she claims to have been the one who expelled the Hyksos and finally created order in the land—in all certainty, a total lie.

"I have never slept, like one who neglects his duty, but have restored what lay in ruins. I have raised up that which had been torn down ever since the time when the Asians were in [their capital] Avaris in the northland, plundering hordes who leveled all that had been built. They ruled without the sun god Re and did not act according to his commands all the way up to my time, when I was placed on Re's throne."

This charge alone against the Hyksos, that "they ruled without the sun god Re," who among other things was the god of justice, clearly reveals the propagandistic quality of the text. That this charge is untrue is one of the few things we know with real certainty about the Hyksos. Most of the Hyksos kings have names which, in traditional Egyptian fashion, incorporate praise of the god Re, like "Great is Re's strength" or "Re is the sword's master." One of them calls himself "Re's beloved son of his flesh" and "Re's living image on earth," and in his victory inscription Kamose still calls his opponent "Re's son, Apophis." If the idea of making this charge had come up in Kamose's time, he would certainly not have used this appellation for the Hyksos king.

Nevertheless, it was a fine idea from a propaganda standpoint, and it was brought up again in a later account which depicts the beginning of the war against the Hyksos.

"Now it came to pass that Egypt's land lay under a plague. There was no lord who was king at that time. And so it was that King Sekenenre was ruler in Thebes, but the plague [i.e., the Hyksos king] was in Avaris, and the whole land was obliged to pay him tribute.

"The Hyksos king Apophis had made the god Sutech supreme and served no other god in the whole land save Sutech."

Sutech was a modified, Asian version of the Egyptian god Seth, the arch foe of the royal god Horus. Apophis was thus a worshiper of Baal, in Old Testament terms, one who had

Woman as Pharaoh—Hatshepsut. About sixteenth century B.C.
Kunstgeschichtliches Seminar, Marburg.

Tutanchamen goes hunting.

Fish from the Red Sea. Detail from relief at Deir el Bahri.

Haremhab offering wine to Anubis. Wall painting from Thebes.

The Anubis Chapel, Hatshepsut's temple, Deir el Bahri. About
sixteenth century B.C. Kunstgeschichtliches Seminar, Marburg.

heretically denied the true supreme god, the sun god Re or Amon-Re.

But the prince of Thebes, Sekenenre, the hero of the story "bowed down before no other god in the land save for Amon-Re, the king of the gods."

The Hyksos ruler now comes up with the idea of sending "an offensive accusation" to Sekenenre, and dispatches a messenger to the prince of Thebes "with the accusation which his writers and wise men had told him."

The charge reads: "Let it be seen to that one gets away from the hippopotamus pool, which is in Thebes, since the hippopotamuses let me sleep neither day nor night, for their roars echo in my ears.

"The prince of Thebes was stricken dumb with wonder and was in a great quandary and did not know how he would answer King Apophis' messenger."

Unfortunately we don't get to learn the end of the story. Scholars, too, have been in a quandary when it comes to finding some plausible explanation for the mysterious message. How could the roars of the hippopotamuses at Thebes disturb the sleep of the Hyksos king in Avaris, about four hundred miles away?

If, however, you consider the role which the hippopotamus played in religion, I think that you can arrive at a reasonable interpretation. The hippopotamus was the symbol for the evil in the world and for Seth, the foe of the gods. We know that in some places in Egypt a ritual drama was acted out, in which the king killed a hippopotamus and thereby defeated evil. Apophis is not concerned with the hippopotamus as such. When he says that one should get away from the hippopotamus pool, he may very well mean simply that the hippopotamuses should be left in peace. What disturbed Apophis' sleep, however, was the roar of the sacred animal of his god Seth, when it was hunted down in a religious rite. This was what echoed in his ears day and night, even though he could not hear it in a literal sense.

With this explanation, the theme of the story becomes consistently the same. On the one side, stands the Hyksos king who only worships the foe of the gods; on the other, the pious Theban prince Sekenenre, the champion of the true religion.

The propaganda against the Hyksos reaches its height in the latest depiction of them, the version which the Egyptian priest Manetho included in his history of Egypt in the third century before Christ.

"We had a King Tutimaios. During his reign, god did not favor us, I know not why, and suddenly men of obscure origin broke into the country from the east and made war on the land, and easily and without a fight they conquered it by force. While they seized the leaders in the land, they also brutally burned the cities and razed the temples of the gods. All the inhabitants were treated with the utmost cruelty, in that they slaughtered some and led away the women and children of others into slavery." After an enumeration of the six most important Hyksos rulers follow the characteristic words: "These six became the first rulers, always drinking and tearing up Egypt by the roots."

Despite the testimony of the contemporary sources and the fact that one can trace how the propaganda mounts and paints in ever-darker colors, it is this version, the latest one, written one and a half thousand years after the rule of the Hyksos, which today still marks the accounts in most modern text-books—truly effective propaganda.

When you make a close inspection of the Egyptian historical texts, you find that some of them are purely conventional descriptions built on certain religious axioms and therefore unalterable in principle. Others can justly be termed propaganda texts, in which the truth is well hidden and often not susceptible to analysis with any sure results. One can see this much: that a propagandistic purpose underlies the text and that the account cannot possibly accord with the truth. You may wonder then how we can ever get a clear picture of the actual historical events. Well, this is certainly not easy sometimes, and it can be done only by comparing many different texts of varied nature. Often you have to content yourself with putting a question mark in the margin of the official Egyptian version.

Convention and propaganda among the ancient Egyptians themselves often prevent modern research from doing full justice to the actors in the drama of history. Especially because of propaganda's slander and flattery, the ancient Egyptian saying must all too often be put to shame:

"The valiant man's reputation rests upon what he has done."

The sacred wedding, and woman
as Pharaoh

In the 1500s before Christ, the Egyptians drove out their
foreign masters, the Hyksos, who had ruled the land for over
a hundred years. Egypt became a warlike nation and a great
power in the Middle East. From the Sudan in the south to
Syria in the north, a great empire was built up under the
leadership of a series of Pharaohs who were outstanding warriors.

The techniques of war had undergone a thorough revision.

Temporary conscription could no longer suffice, and wars were now waged by professional armies. The reason for this change was the introduction of the battle chariot drawn by fiery horses. Spawning new tactics of war, this was a military innovation as important as the dominant role of air power in World War II. Antiquated armies which lacked command of the new techniques were torn apart and crushed when they encountered the new chariot units, which combined maneuverability with great striking power.

It was a difficult weapon to master. To stay on the chariot and to fight from it as it hurtled across uneven ground behind wildly galloping horses was a circus feat which had to be practiced from childhood. We are told that in Egypt the children were taken off to the training grounds when they were no taller than the length of two forearms, though this is probably something of an exaggeration. And so there developed everywhere a military caste of professional soldiers, supported by what might be termed military tenant farms—in other words, plots of land which a family held only so long as one of its members was serving in the army.

At the head of this army stood the king, and hence a new quality became part of the monarchic ideal. The king was also to be a professional soldier, the soldier of soldiers. From childhood he was to be trained in the aristocratic sports of his time—to rein the half-wild chariot horses, to shoot with bow and arrow, to bring down lions and other game with lance and with bow—all as preparation for his tasks in war.

He becomes the eternally young, valiant hero, the foremost of all the nation's heroes in battle. He can shoot arrows through thick sheets of copper, while others must be content with wooden targets. No one else can stretch his bow. When he is out on the Nile in his royal boat and the rowers tire, he rows the great boat by himself farther than the whole crew of oarsmen had strength to do.

This expansion of the king's role as hero in war, this spirit of the professional soldier, is now combined with the old conception of the king as the highest god, as the all-powerful. But the reviving tendency to accord the king an increasingly dominant role comes in conflict with another conception, namely, that of the king as the son of the supreme god, Amon.

During this time Thebes was the imperial capital, and the foremost god of the land was now Thebes' god, Amon. Only he who was Amon's son of his flesh had the right to ascend the throne. But how can a prince be the son of a god, the fruit of his loins? Because he was begotten as the result of a sacred wedding between Amon and the king's great chief consort.

Like all other oriental rulers the Pharaohs had a large harem, and from among the harem women a favorite was chosen to play the role of the divine consort. At this sacred wedding, which we must think of as a festive ritual, the ruling king takes the part of the divine bridegroom, Amon. Of course, he in turn was also the son of Amon's flesh, the fruit of the preceding generation's sacred wedding between Amon and the chief consort. The family relationships under these conditions seem a bit bewildering, and it is rather puzzling how the son could play his own father's role in this context. But such logical objections never particularly bothered ancient Egyptian theology.

Then, too, in theological terms, the whole thing was the other way around. We say profanely that the king appears in the play as the god Amon because in practice he certainly did, but the Egyptian theologian says that it is the god Amon who appears as the ruling king. He believed in the real existence of the god, as we do not.

The sacred wedding follows a mystic, ritual pattern, which extends throughout the Middle East. We find it in the Babylonian-Assyrian area, and again, which is more interesting to us, in the ancient texts from Ras Shamra. In many respects these texts reflect the Canaanitic religion which left such deep impressions on the Old Testament. The motif is also found in the Old Testament itself. Some maintain, probably rightly, that the story of how the aged Sarah, with God's help bore a son for Abraham is based on the concept of the sacred wedding. We should also see against this background the account in Luke of the Annunciation and the birth of Jesus. For the ancients of the East this was the normal pattern for the genesis of one who has been raised above the human, whether he be Pharaoh of Egypt, a king and his people's leader, or a religious savior.

The most complete account of such a sacred wedding is found in the famous temple in Deir el Bahri, on the west bank of the Nile, in the burial ground of the capital city of Thebes. It was Queen Hatshepsut who there built a temple for herself and for the god Amon-Re. This temple is perhaps one of the most brilliant achievements of Egyptian art and architecture. The wonderful white limestone colonnades of the terraces harmonize with the natural setting, the great mountain massif against which the temple rises. The feeling that grips you, as you wander about in this temple, can be compared only with the unforgettable impression made on every Westerner by a visit to the storied Acropolis of Athens, with all that place, rightly or wrongly, symbolizes.

That this particular temple should have an unusually detailed representation of the sacred wedding was dictated by political expediency. It was due to the fact that the eighteenth dynasty had such bad luck with the order of succession to the throne. The premise for its normal functioning was, of course, that the child born after the sacred wedding would be a boy and that he would outlive his parents. Even if the sacred wedding were repeated, things might go so badly that the king never had a son who survived him. This was the case with Hatshepsut's parents; therefore, extraordinary measures had to be taken to arrange the succession in another way. Princess Hatshepsut, born of a divine wedding, was married off to a half-brother, Tuthmosis II, who was the son of one of the king's other wives.

But Hatshepsut had no sons who survived her, only daughters. When her husband died, she became the guardian of the underage prince, Tuthmosis III, who was regarded as heir to the throne, although he was the son of another of the royal wives. Then Hatshepsut seized the opportunity to take power for herself and emerged as king, although a woman. In terms of the succession, it was really only her sex which stood in the way. Otherwise she had full right to the throne, since she was the issue of a sacred wedding. It was, therefore, she who, more fully than anyone else, described the sacred wedding which gave her the right to mount the Pharaoh's throne as ruler.

The ceremony begins with the god Amon informing the other gods that he has decided to beget a new king, a decision which the assembled gods greet with jubilation when they hear what rich offerings and other pious deeds may be expected of the new king.

Then Amon turns to the god of wisdom, Thoth, to get more intimate details about the bride, the great consort of the ruling king, Tuthmosis I. Thoth is full of enthusiasm: "This young woman who you have mentioned . . . Ahmose is her name. She is the most beautiful of all the women in the land."

Amon turns himself into Queen Ahmose's husband, King Tuthmosis I, and goes off to his bride, accompanied by the god Thoth.

"They found her resting amidst the beauty of the palace. The fragrance of the gods woke her, and she smiled at His Majesty. Then he went to her immediately, filled with desire. He gave her his heart and allowed her to see him in his divine form after he had come to her. She rejoiced over his beauty, and love for him coursed through her limbs. The palace was filled with the fragrance of the gods, which was like all the perfumes of Punt, the land of incense."

After completion of the rite, it is the creator god Chnum who forms the child and its personality, which he does like a potter on a potter's wheel. In spite of this method, which seems rather drastically primitive, the result is good. The divine child becomes "better than all the gods."

In another text, the child Hatshepsut is described as follows:

"Her Majesty became greater than all things, more beautiful to view than all things. Her form was that of a god, her character was that of a god. She acted in all things as a god would act, and her splendor was that of a god." She became "Amon's glorious image, his living statue on earth."

When the child had been so shaped in her mother's womb, this child whose glowing future was prophesied and predestined by the god Amon himself at the wedding, the time arrives for Queen Ahmose, the mother of the divine child, to give birth. And as the Lord sends an angel to the Virgin Mary, so Amon sends the god Thoth to Queen Ahmose to foretell the birth of the divine child. With the help of the gods who are specialists in protecting women in childbirth and caring for the newborn, all goes well. The babe is given over to the happy father, Amon, who greets her with these words: "Welcome, welcome in peace, daughter of my flesh, my beloved Hatshepsut. A king are you, who shall wear the royal crowns in eternal possession of the throne of [the royal god] Horus, the living [god]!"

Hatshepsut, in short, used this detailed account of the sacred wedding as a propaganda tract to establish her right of succession to the throne.

But her status as a female regent was delicate in this time of emphasis on the male-warrior ideal, and more propaganda was necessary to maintain her power. In one inscription she says of herself: "For me were prophesied many years as a born conqueror. I have come as the uraeus serpent of the royal god Horus, which spits fire against the enemy."

That the Egyptian king should be "a born conqueror" was demanded by both the royal ideal of the time and the ever-present latent dangers inherent in Egypt's foreign relations. As a woman, Hatshepsut can never fully correspond to this ideal, even though she usually has herself portrayed in art as a man of athletic build. In another category of statues she permits more of her femininity to appear, and these statues emphasize her likeness to her family's ancestral mother, the first "great royal consort."

Of course, the ace of trumps in Hatshepsut's hand was that she, unlike the male pretenders to the throne, was descended in direct line from the great consort. The others, who were only children of ancillary wives, had no divine blood in their veins; therefore only she had the right by blood to the throne. Therefore, the portraits which emphasized her similarity to her ancestral mother were certainly also conscious political propaganda against her rivals for the throne.

It is impossible to tell how Hatshepsut really looked. The various pictures of her show completely different features.

Understandably Hatshepsut usually passes over her warlike deeds with eloquent silence. This was, after all, her great weakness as a king, that she could never personally lead an Egyptian army in the field, as her times demanded. In the temple at Deir el Bahri, where she portrayed her great accomplishments in words and pictures, triumphs on the fields of battle would conventionally also have been represented. Propaganda, however, has to have some basis of truth and, in any case, ought not to put its finger on the sore point. Therefore, next to the depiction of the sacred wedding, the main attraction had to be a trade expedition to the land of Punt to bring back the incense and myrrh needed for the cult of the gods.

An expedition to this far-off land really was an exploit. From the city of Thebes the route led first across the desert down to the Red Sea, where the boats were built. Then followed the seemingly endless voyage on one of the world's hottest seas. The boats were so constructed that they had to sail close to the shore line, despite the dangerous reefs which were scattered along the coast. The ships could only sail before the wind. When the wind blew from the sides or against them, or when the wind died down, the heavy vessels had to be rowed beneath the burning sun. There were also long barren stretches between the places on the coast where fresh water could be obtained. And so the voyage went, all the way down to Somaliland, where we can probably place the legendary Punt, the home of the sought-after incense trees.

This was an impressive performance in every way, but Hatshepsut's inscriptions made it into a heroic deed which would have been unheard-of for her forefathers and which no one could have dreamed of accomplishing. If one goes through the Egyptian records of expeditions to Punt, the picture is quite different. Almost every Egyptian ruler had made such an expedition, but only Hatshepsut presents it as something remarkable. The others had different and, in their view, more notable things to recount. They mention only in passing that they, too, sent expeditions to Punt. Hatshepsut, however, made it her great piece of propaganda, and succeeded so well that nearly all modern history books still speak with the highest respect of this expedition, as though it were a unique achievement.

In still another area Hatshepsut described her accomplishments in greater detail than the other Pharaohs—here, too, perhaps, with some propagandistic purpose.

– In the great Amon temple at Karnak in Thebes, she put up two obelisks, of which one still stands in the same place today. Obelisks, of course, are colossal four-sided pillars, hewn from a single block of granite and coming to a point in the shape of a pyramid at the top. The largest ones are almost one hundred feet in length—or, if you prefer, height—and about six feet wide, and weigh about three hundred and fifty tons. Throughout time they have fascinated succeeding generations both because of their size and because of their beauty of material and purity of line. They rise against the sky as supreme triumphs of architectural genius over a recalcitrant material. –

With infinite pains Roman emperors transported Egyptian obelisks to Constantinople and Rome, and during the last century one was taken to London, one to Paris, and one across the Atlantic to New York. When you consider the cost of transporting these obelisks in modern times (the moving cost for the New York obelisk, even then, was over $125,000), and when you read that modern engineers have had great difficulties in handling the obelisks, you must wonder how the ancient

View from the shrine of Hatshepsut's temple at
Deir el Bahri through the granite portal toward the Nile.
About sixteenth century B.C.

Musicians. Wall painting from Thebes.

22916

Egyptians managed, when they had neither the jackscrew nor even a real block and tackle.

Judging by Egyptian texts, the Egyptians themselves didn't think that the technical problems were so formidable. Of all the rulers who raised obelisks, and there were many, only Hatshepsut has left a detailed account in pictures of their actual transportation from the stone quarries to their final destinations.

With the aid of her description and a number of other sources we can get an approximate picture of how the whole process was managed. In my own view, at least, this is one of the most fascinating feats of ancient Egyptian engineering, so let us try to reconstruct, in more detail, the work on Queen Hatshepsut's obelisks.

A little over a mile from Aswan, the real Egypt's southernmost city, down by the first Nile fall, lie the stone quarries out in the desert. There great bonfires have been lit to heat up the granite. Then when cold water is poured on the heated surface, the stone splits apart in small pieces. The laborers work loose the crumbled surface with round, fist-sized stones of a still harder material, dolerite. Large layers are removed in this fashion in order to get down to the fresh stone below the surface cracks. At a certain point, they thought that they had come down far enough, that they could now carve out a faultless obelisk about one hundred feet long.

The workers are spread out within an area marked off with red paint, in order to hack out the obelisk with the balls of dolerite. The stonecutters are put to work, stationed as close together as possible without getting in one another's way. Some work on the flat, horizontal surface, which will form one side of the obelisk; others dig vertically in a groove about half a yard wide. The sun beats down unmercifully on the naked, sweating bodies, but the overseers' whips permit no rest. Slowly but surely the hard granite is crumbled apart, and the obelisk begins to take form.

Anxiously watchful eyes follow their progress. Look, there

is a crack in the stone! Is it only a surface crack, or does it continue on through, so that they will never be able to carve out a perfect obelisk and all their work will have gone for naught? Specialists are sent over to dig test cavities and to follow the crack downward. The stone dust makes it difficult to see precisely how things are, and the surface has to be polished constantly so that the experts can really study the structure of the crack.

Every possible precautionary measure has been taken, but one day they strike a crack which simply continues down, straight through the half-completed obelisk. No alternative remains. With death in his heart, the work foreman must decide to begin all over again in a new spot. As a monument to his lack of skill, the uncompleted obelisk will lie there for thousands of years, and there is no comfort for him in the fact that, thanks to this, archeologists in later times will be able to understand the process of carving out an obelisk.

The fate of this foreman does not invite emulation, and his error may not be repeated. At last, the workers succeed to the point where an obelisk lies ready, except for the underside. From the grooves along the sides, the stonecutters begin to work their way in under the enormous mass of granite. If their labor was hard and heavy before, it is now inhuman. Each one hacks out a narrow passageway under the obelisk, and when a channel is finished, stones are packed in to provide a new support for the obelisk. The last remnants of the original stone bed are cut away. Will the packing hold, or will the workers now chipping their way beneath this stone weighing three hundred and fifty tons be crushed when the packing gives way? And how will they manage to shift this mass to the great wooden sledge on which the obelisk will be pulled down to the river?

It seems miraculous, but they succeed. A couple of thousand workers are now harnessed to the sledge, and the colossal stone begins to glide forward slowly on the roadway of clay bricks which has been built down to the river. This road continues all the way to the ship in the harbor. Almost two hundred feet long and some sixty feet wide, the ship stands in dry dock, propped up by large beams and mounds of earth. When the obelisk is on board, the water is let into the dry dock, lifting the ship.

Now nine galleys, each with thirty-two rowers, take the barge in tow. As jubilant throngs look on, they begin the triumphal journey to Thebes, the capital city. Danger is a constant on the difficult waterways of the Nile, with sand bars continually changing position. Running aground can be avoided only if the pilots on the escort vessels exercise the utmost vigilance. Should the boat with the obelisk run aground, no power on earth could budge its weight, with the strong current immediately packing new sand masses around it.

But now the boat lands in the harbor of the capital, in the dry dock readied for it, and the obelisk is pulled up on the ramp of clay bricks, which extends all the way to the entrance of the great temple of the royal god Amon.

Now comes the most difficult feat of all—to set the obelisk in place as a perpendicular. The brick ramp slants slowly upward, until in front of the temple door it rises sixty-five feet above ground level, over the foundation stone on which the obelisk is to stand. The top surface of this stone has been leveled with the utmost precision to make it absolutely horizontal. Directly above the foundation stone there is a funnel-shaped, oblong hole in the ramp, and this hole is filled with sand.

Thousands of workers haul the obelisk up the ramp far enough so that its lower portion rests on the loose sand and its upper portion rests on the solid brick ramp. Now they begin to empty out the sand, through underground passages inside the ramp. The bottom of the obelisk sinks lower and lower, while the top still rests on the ramp. Finally the obelisk pitches forward and stands firmly on its foundation.

The calculations were correct, the wonder has been performed, and the stone giant stands straight up in place. The ramp is dug away, and in a festive ceremony Queen Hatshepsut rewards the proud foreman of the work and dedicates the new wonder to the land's highest god. The queen's address to "all those who in coming years shall behold Her Majesty's monument," can be incribed on the podium:

"As truly as I live, as truly as the sun god loves me . . . these two obelisks, which I adorned with silver-gold for my father Amon, so that my name shall live on in this temple for eternities' eternity, they are of one block of strong granite without joint or seam. I permitted the work to go on from the fifteenth year of my rule, the first day of the second month of winter, to the sixteenth year, the last day of the third month of floods." (This makes seven months from the start of work in the stone quarry.) "I did this for Him for the sake of my heart's integrity, as a king for a god."

That Queen Hatshepsut, despite all these real or pretended accomplishments, was widely hated we can surmise from monuments from her own time. Her favorite, Senmut, who was probably the creator of the wonderful Deir el Bahri temple, seems to have guessed what the future would bring. He had been allowed to build himself a noble grave, with colonnades which faced his architectural masterpiece, Hatshepsut's temple. But as though he had known that he would not be permitted to rest in peace in this grave, after his powerful protectress had died, he secretly made himself another grave, hidden deep down under the walls which surrounded the temple itself.

In still another way he tried to prevent his name from being effaced and forgotten when the political situation changed. In the chapel of the temple he had himself pictured on the entrance wall, just inside the door. He could then be sure that no one would deface the pictures so long as the cult was maintained in the temple, simply because no one would see them. The only one permitted to enter the chapel was the officiating priest. The priest was required to fix his eyes upon the picture of the god the entire time. He would therefore never discover that Senmut, in a way which Egyptians would regard as blasphemous, had let himself be immortalized in the holiest place of all.

When Hatshepsut died and the great war leader Tuthmosis III, her ward, ascended the throne, memories of the queen and of her favorites were blotted out wherever possible. The beautiful statues of the queen which graced the Deir el Bahri temple were smashed and hurled down into a stone quarry. Everywhere the queen's hateful name was effaced. In its place Tuthmosis put either his own name or the name of the king who had ruled before Hatshepsut, to imply unbroken continuity. All those who had faithfully served the woman on the throne also had their names effaced from the graves which they had built with the very purpose, among others, that their "names would live eternally."

Hatshepsut's reign was treated by her successors on the throne as though it had never existed. Here the question of propaganda is hardly involved any longer. This is the purposeful and total eradication of the past by a present which it did not suit.

Tuthmosis III, antiquity's Napoleon

"Enemy troops have invaded through the Sinai desert and have reached the eastern part of the Delta."

Since time immemorial the Egyptians knew that when this report came—and it came often in the millenniums of Egypt's history—the land's survival as an independent state was at stake.

The Sinai desert lies as a barrier between Egypt and her neighbors in the northeast. When the enemy had successfully passed it, the prospects for effective resistance were slight. The struggle then moved on into the densely populated region of the Nile Valley itself, and even if the Egyptians succeeded in driving back their attackers, it cost them great sacrifices among the civilian population.

When the Pharaoh Tuthmosis III seized power in Egypt, in

the year 1483 B.C., the land found itself, as in so many other periods before and after, in this dangerous predicament. All the smaller realms of Palestine and Syria had formed a coalition against Egypt, and this league was supported by a major power in the interior of Syria, near the upper reaches of the Tigris and Euphrates rivers. This was the new state of Mitanni, a military state equipped with the most modern military resources of the time and governed by an Indo-European ruling caste. The earlier Egyptian dominion in Palestine and Syria had already been wiped out, and the enemy's troops now threatened the borders of Egypt itself.

How had it come to this? Only a generation before, Tuthmosis III's grandfather, Tuthmosis I, had controlled Syria and Palestine and had managed to push forward with an army all the way to the upper Euphrates. And still twenty-two years before Tuthmosis III's assumption of power, Egypt was not threatened by any danger from the north.

But then, it was twenty-two years earlier, that developments catastrophic for the country had begun.

The Pharaoh Tuthmosis II had just died. He had been a sickly and weak ruler, but during his short reign the situation had not had time to deteriorate. Respect for Egypt still lingered on from the earlier kings' forceful interventions in Asian trouble spots. The burning issue in domestic politics at the death of Tuthmosis II was who his successor would be. Only a prince borne by the chief royal consort had the right to ascend the throne, and there was no such prince. Tuthmosis II and his chief consort, Hatshepsut, had had only two daughters.

In this situation the priests of the supreme god, Amon, intervened by means of an oracle.

This took place at a festival in the great Amon temple at Karnak. The temple courts were filled with worshipful throngs, and in the pillared halls stood the lower priesthood. Among them was the young Prince Tuthmosis, the son of one of the concubines of the late king. He was still only a child and had not yet attained any great priestly station. Then a procession carried forward the divine image of Amon in a golden chair, borne high over the multitude on the shoulders of chosen priests and preceded by head priests with incense offerings.

"The god neared his temple, illuminating heaven and earth with his beauty . . . His glowing rays struck the eyes of the people like a sunrise," a contemporary account tells us.

But when the offerings to the god had been made, the traditional ritual was suddenly interrupted.

"[The god] began to move around on both sides of the hall of pillars," Tuthmosis tells us, "and they who were before him did not understand what he was doing, when he was looking for me everywhere. Then he recognized me and stopped [in front of me] . . . I threw myself on the ground before him, but he raised me up and installed me in the king's place in the temple . . . The god himself placed me [on the throne], and I was adorned with the crowns which were upon his head."

And thus the god himself—in other words, the statue directed by his priests—had chosen the small prince, the son of a concubine of the nation's ruler. He was crowned Pharaoh, the third to bear the name Tuthmosis.

But since he was underage, he himself could not rule. His stepmother, the great royal consort Hatshepsut, took advantage of this fact to seize the power for herself.

Under her rule everything seems to have gone well at first, and there was contentment in the land. But then threatening clouds began to gather in Palestine and Syria. Hatshepsut could not deal with the dangers from without. As a woman, she could hardly place herself at the head of an army and put a brake on the increasing aggressiveness of the Asians. Province after province withdrew from Egyptian control, and even within the country opposition made itself felt. Her most trusted adviser, Senmut, was forced out, but the trend could no longer be checked.

Tuthmosis III had now grown up, but he could still be held back for a time from intervention in the increasingly dangerous course of events. Whether he had been taken into custody, we do not know; we can only see that now his name was never mentioned in the official documents.

Then at last his hour struck, fully twenty-two years after his official ascension to the throne. Hatshepsut, his deeply hated stepmother, disappeared from the political arena—whether she died a natural death or was done away with is not known—and Tuthmosis III could act after his long wait. Shortly after his assumption of power the Egyptian army set off for Palestine to crush the great alliance of Syrian-Palestinian princes, supported by the major power, Mitanni, far to the north.

They first encountered resistance a short distance beyond the Palestine border. The enemy had concentrated its forces at the city of Megiddo. Now ensued the first battle in history to be fought near this city, which was so often to be the scene of decisive conflicts. "We stand at Armageddon [Megiddo]" is still a familiar phrase in our own language, although a bit old-fashioned now. What is remarkable about Tuthmosis III's battle at Megiddo is not only that it was the first in the long series of battles there, but also that it is the first battle in history which we can follow in some detail.

Megiddo lies at the southern end of the great plain which extends across Palestine from Haifa on the Mediterranean to the Valley of Jordan, just south of the Sea of Galilee. South of Megiddo lie the lower reaches of Carmel's high mountains, and when you approach it from the south, there are only three routes to follow. One makes a crook to the north and comes out on the plain north of Megiddo; another, the easiest route, curves to the east and comes out on the plain south of Megiddo. But, in addition, there is a narrow and arduous pathway through the mountains which heads directly for the city.

Which route would the Egyptian army choose?

The king holds a council of war with his generals. He suggests they should move straight forward against Megiddo by the shortest route. His advisers are completely amazed by his foolhardy idea and do all they can to dissuade the king:

"The road is small and impassable! We will march, horse be-

hind horse, man behind man, and our advance troops will
have to fight before the rear guard can move up! There are
two other routes. May our lord choose whichever of these he
wills, but let us not take the most impassable road!"

But Tuthmosis II stands by his decision:

"I swear by the sun god Re . . . I shall follow this route!
Let him do as he wills, he who wishes to take the other roads
you speak of and he who wishes to follow me. Shall the enemy
whom Re abominates say: 'Does His Majesty go another way?
He must be getting frightened of us!' "

Then the generals give up their resistance:

"We shall follow Your Majesty wherever he may go, for
surely a servant's place is behind his master!"

And so begins the long and difficult march through the mountains, horse behind horse, man behind man. The king's daring
plan succeeds beyond all expectations. The enemy, the three
hundred and thirty princes and their troops, had never dreamed
that the Egyptian forces would choose this direct route to the
city, dangerous and almost impassable for an army. They had,
therefore, concentrated their forces near the easily traversed
southern route. The whole Egyptian army is able to get through
the mountain pass and range itself for battle before the enemy
has time to regroup. Since night had fallen during these troop
movements, the armies first engage the next morning.

The main body of the Egyptian forces now hurtles forward,
not against the enemy troops, but against the city of Megiddo
itself, and threatens to take it by storm. Once again a totally
unexpected maneuver has taken the enemy by surprise, and
they set off in a headlong race for the city to prevent the storm-
ing and to take refuge within the walls.

The gates of the city close, and the last refugees from the
battlefield have to be hauled over the walls by means of im-
provised ropes made by tying clothes together.

"If only the army had not devoted itself now to plundering
the belongings of the enemy [left on the battle field], the city
of Megiddo could have been captured at that moment, when

the prince of the city of Kadesh and the prince of Megiddo itself had to be hauled hastily into the city."

So the Egyptian historian describes the situation. As though to comfort his Egyptian readers, he goes on to enumerate all the riches, particularly horses and chariots decorated with gold and silver, which the Egyptians took as spoils from the battle-field—"where the enemy's champions lay scattered like fish on a shoal," as the text forcefully puts it.

But the consequence of this breach of discipline at the crucial moment was that Megiddo fell only after seven months of siege, although completely enclosed by the Egyptian army, which had built a fortified wall around the entire city. Starved out, the inhabitants finally had to surrender, and rich spoils fell into Egyptian hands.

The enemy were allowed to go free, but under humiliating circumstances. Their horses and chariots, weapons which were indispensable in warfare of the times and were tactically and strategically comparable to the armored vehicles of modern times, had to be turned over to the Egyptians, leaving them to wend their way home ignominiously on the back of donkeys. Furthermore, they had to swear an oath by all that was holy to them that they would never again take up arms against the Egyptians.

But such international agreements were worth no more in their time than in our own, and the war was by no means over, despite the great initial victory and the forced oath of peace.

At Megiddo, Tuthmosis III had shown himself capable of swift and bold action, winning victory by seizing the iniative from the enemy. Now a task remained that demanded all the perseverance and patience he had learned during the long period of passivity his stepmother had forced upon him.

There could never be any lasting peace or security until northern Syria and its leader, the prince of Kadesh, had been subdued, and until a hard blow had also been dealt to Mitanni, the great power which supported him in the fight against Egypt. To attain these goals required years of preparation and pre-

Unfinished obelisk in the stone quarry of Aswan.

Hatshepsut's obelisk in the temple at Karnak.
About sixteenth century B.C.

Tuthmosis III's pillars at Karnak. Fifteenth century B.C.

One of the two colossi of Amenophis III at Thebes.
About fifteenth century B.C.

liminary military operations. If the conflict at Megiddo is the first battle in history of which details are known, the farsighted policy of Tuthmosis III is the first instance of grand strategy which we can trace in history.

It proved impossible to get sufficiently far north during the favorable time of year, if the army had to march the long and difficult land route through the Sinai desert and all the way up through Palestine and Syria. Tuthmosis III, therefore, decided upon a large-scale amphibious operation, the first we know of.

The preparations began with conquest by land of all the Syrian coastal cities, thereby making resistance on the sea also impossible for the enemy. The Egyptians held complete command of the ocean. The invasion fleet was built in the harbor of Perunefer, in the vicinity of modern Cairo.

By chance, a few of the accounts kept by the shipyards have been preserved. From these it appears that the ships were primarily transports, since there was no reason to expect any sea battles.

Finally, after five years of preparations, everything was ready for the great amphibious operation. The army was shipped directly to the north Syrian port which lies closest to the main objective, the city of Kadesh, in the interior of the country. After a rapid march over the high coastal mountains the Egyptians succeeded in taking the city by storm. This victory opened the way for the great final thrust against the kingdom of Mitanni, on the other side of the Euphrates.

Like a cautious general, however, Tuthmosis III first devoted still another year to strengthening his naval base, and only then did he proceed, in the eighth year of his campaign. City after city in the interior of northern Syria fell. The army was transported over the Euphrates by boats built on the Syrian coast solely for this purpose and pulled along on wagons over high mountains, endless steppes, and desert regions. The Egyptian forces ravaged the western part of the great Mitanni kingdom, but they were not up to crushing it.

Despite the years of carefully planned preparations, the

distance from Egypt was still too great, and the resources of
the time were too limited to permit a crushing blow to be dealt
so far from home bases. Palestine and Syria could be held effectively by occupation, but when it proved impossible to elim-
inate Mitanni, it was also impossible to pacify the northernmost
parts of Syria, which could always draw renewed support from
Mitanni.

Once again the Egyptian forces had to move against the city
of Kadesh, and there they almost came to grief. Just at the decisive moment, when the Egyptian chariots were ranged for
attack, the prince of Kadesh set loose a mare in heat against
the Egyptian lines. The mare galloped in among the neighing
war stallions, and the whole chariot formation was about to
be torn up before the resourceful general, Amenemheb, could
intervene. He leapt from his chariot and managed to catch up
with the mare and kill her. It would certainly have been an
irony of fate if the plans and labors of so many years had come
to naught because of a mare.

From the time he took power, Tuthmosis III seems to have
spent his whole life in the field. The recreation he permitted
himself was hunting dangerous game. In Syria he dispatched
no fewer than one hundred twenty elephants and was nearly
killed by the largest of them. In the Nubian province to the
south, which he also inspected during a long trip, he amused
himself by hunting lions. Once when he downed a rhinoceros,
rare in that region even then, it was considered so remarkable
an achievement that the rhinoceros got his portrait on the wall
of a temple, with a typical hunter's detailed account of all his
measurements.

In the southern part of the empire which Tuthmosis managed
to build up, from the interior of the Sudan in the south to
present-day Turkey's southern border, the native Nubian population was completely Egyptianized, and the Egyptians could
draw freely on the province's rich raw materials, gold and
colonial products.

In Palestine and Syria, it was not that easy. Despite all the non-aggression pacts, despite a highly refined system of holding the children of princes as hostages in Egypt, and despite the numerous Egyptian garrisons, the will to resist remained unbroken. Tuthmosis III's successors also had to fight many battles there. But Egypt's border in the northeast was effectively protected by this zone of subjugated lands, and there was no need to fear that the country's existence would be threatened by invasions through Palestine, the constant danger for Egypt.

These are the outer aspects of the life of Tuthmosis III, who built up the first great Egyptian empire, and who has been called "Antiquity's Napoleon" because of his military aptitude, even genius.

But what was he like as a person?

There is one more feature which we can add to the picture. He owed a debt of gratitude to the god Amon, whose priests had chosen him successor to the throne, and he showed this gratitude by assigning to the god not only large portions of his rich spoils of war, but also whole countries and cities in the Asian provinces.

When the victorious Tuthmosis III returned to the capital from his campaigns he was hailed by Amon-Re in the Temple of Amon in Karnak with the following hymn:

It is Amon-Re who speaks, Karnak's lord:
You have come to me rejoicing when you behold my beauty,
You, my avenging son, Tuthmosis, who lives for eternity.
Out of love for you, I show myself in my bright rays.
My heart is filled with joy over your coming to my temple,
  and my hands grant your limbs protection and life.

A wonder have I wrought for you:
I give you victorious strength against all foreign highlands.
I let your power and fear of you spread through all lowlands,
  Terror of you extends to the four pillars of the sky.
I make your reputation great among all men.
I let Your Majesty's battle cry sound among the barbarians.

The princes of all foreign lands you hold in your hand.
It is I who stretch out my hands and capture them for you.
Nubians in the south I bind together like sheaves by the
thousands and the ten thousands,
And the people of the north are taken captive by the hundred
thousands.
I let your opponents fall beneath your foot soles.
Troublemakers you trample under your feet.
For the earth in all its length and breadth I have delivered
over to you,
East and West are under your supervision.
Joyously you forge ahead through nations.
In your time no one dares to attack.
For I am the one who leads you, so that you meet them.
The waters of the land of two floods you have crossed
with strength and force which I have given you.
They hear your battle cry and flee into their dens,
Of the breath of life have I deprived them,
With terror of you have I filled their hearts.

The king's officials and officers usually also served as priests
of the god, and under Tuthmosis' rule there is never any conflict between the priesthood and the king's men—between
church and state, as it were. This opposition is otherwise one
of the main strands in the internal politics of Egypt, and that
it is now bridged testifies to the power of the royal diplomacy
on the domestic plane as well.

And the individual, the man Tuthmosis III?

His portraits show us an energetic, strong-willed face with
a forceful, eagle nose, but in art individuality is also hidden
under accepted aesthetic norms. So it is with all the other
sources which might cast light on Tuthmosis III as an individual. We can only build our conception of him on depictions
of his outward accomplishments as a warrior and a statesman.
It is usually an illusion to think that you can analyze or characterize a particular individual in ancient Egyptian history.

All such things are hidden behind idealistic pictures and behind religious and political conventions which portray the king as the divine ruler, the son and image of the gods, whose projects can only prosper.

But in the case of Tuthmosis III we have a definite feeling that behind the official panegyrics lurks a strong personality and one of antiquity's most remarkable men, even if he can be glimpsed only as a diffuse but impressive figure in a semi-darkness which inadequate historical sources cannot pierce.

Our estimation is supported by the high regard in which he was held by succeeding generations. When in a later time the Asian provinces have once again been lost, the vassals who remain true to Egypt recall the happy time when the strong hand of Tuthmosis III ruled over land and sea. And for centuries his name was used as almost a magic formula on scarabs, those seals which every important Egyptian used as his mark. Hundreds, perhaps even thousansd of such scarabs, bear witness to the fact that the Egyptians themselves, like historians of our time, regarded Tuthmosis III as one of Egypt's greatest rulers.

Akhenaton — a strange interlude

The latter part of the period in which the eighteenth dynasty ruled Egypt was marked by an increasingly bitter conflict between two factions in domestic politics, between what we might term church and state. On one side stood the king, supported by the military, the great class of professional soldiers which came into being with the introduction of complex chariot warfare. On the other side were the priests of the realm's supreme god, Amon. Through their influence over the royal succession and their role in placing the powerful Tuthmosis III on the throne, the priests had acquired great religious authority and also immeasurable riches, given by the kings—above all, by Tuthmosis III—in gratitude to the god.

In the long run, the king could not tolerate this state within the state, and even the priests of the other gods, completely overshadowed by the dominant position of Amon, had reason to be discontented. Although these priests did not have any real means of launching the struggle, the king did.

Already under the successor to Tuthmosis III, the power struggle between the two, royal authority and the established god, seemed to have begun. On the surface peace was maintained, and we can really only infer that the land had begun to seethe with intrigues. When Amenophis III came to power, the third king after Tuthmosis III, we get the first real evidence that the king was making serious efforts to free himself from the stewardship of the Amon priests.

He began to stress his own divinity in a manner unusual in the past. The royal statues in the temples were to be regarded as independent gods. They became subjects of a divine cult, and in pictures we can see that even the king himself was making offerings to his own statues. We have seen earlier how the statue of Amon was regarded as a living incarnation of the god, which could pick out and crown Tuthmosis III. From this, we can understand what it meant when the royal statues now also became deities, acting independently.

Much later, in the fourth century after Christ, a Latin writer, the Gnostic Asclepius, gives us a picture of what the statue cult could be like in a pagan society. Standing all around in Egypt's temples, he tells us, there are divine idols which perform the most glorious miracles, heal the sick and suffering, interpret dreams and foretell the future. These gods, which ultimately outrank the heavenly gods who, after all, have no real bodies, are created and shaped by human hands. The human creatures have discovered the essential nature of the gods and have been able to reproduce it. By magical arts and sacred rituals they have forced demons and powers to reside in these images, which thus become alive and capable of action.

We have good reason to assume that the essence of this faith already existed in the time of Amenophis III. To some extent, this faith has lived on even into our own times. There is a statue of Ramses II, a king who with the same purpose as Amenophis III set up miraculous statues of himself, and to this ancient statue Egyptian peasant women in modern times still turned for help in sorrow and trouble. In short, so strong was this belief that it could survive despite the contrary teachings of both Christianity and Islam.

Through this "statue policy" Amenophis III tried to approach the old station which the king had had in the time of the pyramids—that of a god who was self-sufficient, not dependent upon the supreme god of the land. But he did not dare to take this final step, and he kept on being the son of the god nevertheless, like his family's rulers before him.

Even though this led to nothing decisive, it was a thrust against the priests of Amon. No doubt they looked with mixed feelings upon the enormous statues of the king being raised in various places. Those now most famous, the so-called Colossi of Memnon, certainly did not inspire in them the same enthusiastic admiration felt by the children of later times.

But this was only one of many challenges to the opposing faction. Heretofore, the high priest of Amon had always been the foremost priest in Upper Egypt, the head of all the priests there, regardless of which gods they served. Amenophis III appointed a prince to be chief of the priests of Upper Egypt but did not at the same time appoint him high priest of Amon in Thebes. Instead, he made him high priest of the god Ptah in Memphis. Such an appointment was a direct attack upon the supremacy of Amon and his priests.

As though this were not enough, at the court they now also began to worship a new god, the sun disk Aton, who would later topple Amon-Re, "the king of the gods," from his position of power.

Amenophis III broke with traditions in yet another way. He took a woman not of royal birth as his great chief consort and thereby designated her as the mother of his successor on the throne. Her name was Tiye, and it was she who gave birth to Akhenaton, Amenophis III's successor.

Akhenaton—or Amenophis, as he was called in his child-hood—and his future consort, Nefertiti, grew up in a time filled with inner conflicts, a time in which the old and the new were splitting apart. The old revered traditions from the days of the great Tuthmosis III had been loosened more and more. Foreign elements had left their marks on Egyptian culture; the supremacy of Amon-Re, "the king of the gods," formerly self-evident, had begun to be questioned. The divine isolation and exalted status of the king and the royal family had been altered fundamentally when Amenophis III had designated the commoner Tiye as the mother of the royal heir.

The struggle with the priesthood of Amon had begun, but Amenophis III withdrew. As he grew older, he lived a pleasant life as a pasha in his harem and otherwise interested himself in hunting and other amusements. He was not the man to carry through a revolution, whether in the political sphere or in the religious.

But Akhenaton was a soul on fire regarding good and evil, a glowing fanatic, filled with the new ideas of the time. And his position as absolute ruler gave him power to realize his slightest whim.

During the initial period of his rule he still retained his original name, Amenophis—which means "Amon is satisfied"—and he did not disturb the old order. To be sure, he worshiped the new god Aton, but still in traditional ways, and all the Egyptian gods, including Amon-Re, received their respective portions of the royal offerings.

Then came his first challenge—the first slap in the faces of Amon's priests and of all conservative circles in Egypt. In Amon-Re's centuries-old temple at Karnak, the enemy's stronghold, Akhenaton had a large temple built to the new god Aton. This was a sun god of the same type as the god Re in the city of Heliopolis, and many of the religious beliefs which the priests

Central aisle of the temple at Luxor. In the foreground,
the colonnade of Amenophis III. Fifteenth century B.C.

Statue of Akhenaton at Karnak. Fourteenth century B.C.

in Heliopolis connected with their god were now launched by
Akhenaton as the teachings of the new god. Heliopolis' priests
of Re had undoubtedly urged on the young king and had
energetically supported him in his rejection of Amon. The god
Re had once been the kingdom's pre-eminent god, but Amon
had outrivaled him. Formerly the priests of Re and not of
Amon had directed the religious life, and the Re priests longed
for revenge. But Aton, the new god to whom they lent support,
would also surpass their old god Re.

The new Aton shrine was a challenge to tradition, and not
only because it was built in Amon's temple. Its design was also
revolutionary. The pillars in the temple were shaped like images
of Akhenaton, as he now called himself, in place of Amenophis.
The king was now no longer named "Amon is satisfied," but
instead "Useful to Aton." These new images of Pharaoh must
have been an abomination in the eyes of all the old believers.

The king should be an ideal figure—an athletically built,
eternally young, divine hero, the foremost of the nation's warriors. But Akhenaton was now portrayed in a manner that
broke purposely with the proud traditions of the rulers who had
transformed peaceful peasants into warriors and conquered an
entire world.

Pharaoh stands there with bent back, a little potbelly, narrow shoulders, womanly thighs, and strengthless arms. The
thin neck can barely hold up the misshapen head, enormously
extended at the back. The face has an unforgettable expression
of burning fanaticism, with its lips twisted in derision. All of the
images seem to be smiling a mocking challenge to Amon.

A new art had made its entry into Egypt. Truth was its motto,
but the truth was whatever Pharaoh dictated. These exaggerated, even blasphemous images of the king must have been
a shock to everyone, a worse shock than any work of modern
art has ever been able to achieve in more recent times.

The priesthood remonstrated strongly. "They let me hear
worse things than any earlier king has had to hear," says
Akhenaton in one inscription. The atmosphere in Thebes, the

stronghold of conservatism, became oppressive, unbearable for the king and his followers. The new required a new setting.

So Akhenaton decided to abandon the old capital city, the heart of the empire. This was a fateful decision. For the Egyptians, the capital was more than an administrative center. It was also a center of religion, of even greater importance to their religious life than, for example, Vatican City is for Catholics. This was the oldest place in the world, the very spot on earth where, at the time of the Creation, the unfathomable, infinite, and absolute divine power had first revealed itself in all its might, and created the world.

This whole tradition was now to be slashed. Akhenaton chose a new location for the capital city, near the present-day El Amarna in Middle Egypt.

He traveled there in his golden chariot. Surrounded by the important men of the realm, he made offerings to the new god Aton, and from the mountain ridge he looked out over the uninhabited plain on which Aton's new city would be built. As in a vision, he saw his creation before his eyes. He raised his arms toward the sun, and in front of the great men he proclaimed his fateful decision.

"Behold Aton's horizon city, which Aton wished should be built as a monument bearing his name.

"No noble advised me, no man in the entire land told me this. No, it was Aton himself, my father, who urged me to build this horizon city—Akhetaton.

"No one else has determined its location. No, you see, it was I, Pharaoh, who did this. I found that this place belonged to no god or goddess, to no prince or princess—no one can lay claim to it.

"As truly as Aton, my father, lives, he who controls life and confers it, he, my father, who permits me to reflect upon eternity and who bears witness of infinity.

"He who created himself as no artist could have created him— he who each day goes up in the East and down in the West, and who never ceases creation in heaven and on earth. Each and every one he keeps alive, and permits me every day to content my eyes with the sight of him, when he shines forth in his temple in the horizon city, after having cloaked his limbs in beautiful rays of love.

"For Aton, my father, shall I build his horizon city in this place . . . Never shall I say, 'I am abondoning Aton's horizon city and going hence to build another handsome dwelling.'

"To my father Aton I shall build shrines and temples in this city. A royal palace shall I raise there. And in the mountains east of the city, a grave shall be prepared for me, so that I may be buried there after countless reigning years which Aton will grant me, and so that the great Queen Nefertiti after countless years may be buried there and so also the royal daughter Meritaton.

"But if I should die in another city—south or north, east or west—then shall I be brought here to be buried in Aton's horizon city!"

The king had made his decision. The new city would be built immediately. There Akhenaton wished to live and die. Multitudes of workers were directed to the spot, a wide desert plain on the shores of the Nile, framed by the steep cliffs of the desert mountains, glittering in the sunlight. As though by magic the desert is turned into a smiling idyll. Within a few years the new capital is finished.

In the harbor traffic is lively. Ships from near and far tie up at the quays and unload the luxuries of the world to make life in Aton's horizon city rich and agreeable. Not only Egyptians are bustling about, shouting and laughing, joking and quarreling. Syrians in gaudy caftans and Cretans in short skirts with colorful patterns mix with the retinue of a Negro vassal from darkest Africa.

We wander up to the large main thoroughfare. At the southern end are the fine districts in which it is fashionable to live. Within high garden walls the luxury villas with wonderful

gardens stand in noble isolation from one another. Here lives
the vizier, Nakht; Aton's high priest, Pawah; General Ramose;
the keeper of the royal stables, Ranofer—in short, the cream
of society.

But we shall not ask about their pasts. Pharaoh is no longer
attended by the old noble families. Now there are newcomers,
all those who in their religious devotions have aligned themselves with Akhenaton and his new teachings and who have
accepted with enthusiasm all that is new. And the enthusiasm
has been rewarded.

Let's go in and visit such a family. When the garden gate
is opened by the gatekeeper, looking out from a gatehouse, we
see before us a long path, and in the background an altarpiece
glows with strong colors. It pictures Akhenaton and Nefertiti
under Aton's golden sun disk. Beside it is a pool where birds
are chattering. Reflected in the water are blossoming trees and
beautiful flowers.

To the right is the villa. From the vestibule we enter a loggia
that feels cool and comfortable after the dust and the broiling
sun of the street. Large air vents on the roof permit cooling
breezes from the north to reach the luxurious room. We continue on into the large salon in the middle of the house, with
its rich columns and large dais with comfortable pillows. The
ceiling is high, and light filters in from ornamented lattice
windows.

The servants hurry to and fro with refreshments, most of
which were produced within the house itself. The master of
the house had been given extensive lands on the other side of
the river. It may be a good thing to be self-sufficient; who knows
how long one can count on receiving wares from other sources?
After all, everyone is not equally content with the new conditions in the land. Perhaps different times will come . . .

We look out toward the back of the house. There the servants
live in small barracks, and behind them lie the refuse heaps.
The indigent neighbor who lives in the district in back may

not like this, but if you are in favor with Pharaoh and live on the main street, you don't need to show consideration.

We continue on toward the center of the city, where the public buildings stand. On the way we pass the workshop of the artist Tuthmosis. He lives well. He is in vogue now and gets to make portraits of the king and the queen, the small princesses, and all the important people. The prominent, of course, do not care to sit as models for very long, but Tuthmosis knows how to satisfy his customers. Their portraits must look rather like Akhenaton, with his large head and small neck, his little potbelly and spindly arms and legs. Pharaoh's relatives, of course, are sometimes quite like him. But the others have to be changed to make them so. The sketches can be good likenesses, but they must be reworked to satisfy the customer. In truth, a good likeness is desirable only when portraying Pharaoh himself.

A little farther down the street lies the university, "The House of Life," where young hopefuls develop skills in medicine and theology, mathematics and surveying, and the many other disciplines.

Then there is the foreign office, to which messengers come from Syria and Palestine, bringing clay tablets—letters for "the sun of nations," Akhenaton. The messengers look tired and harried, surprised and indignant over life in the horizon city. Why? We do not have time to ask them. Trumpet blasts sound through the streets. The king is coming! Everyone steps aside. First the city's corpulent police chief comes running, perspiring and out of breath but proud of this privileged task. Nubians and Asians with spears and cudgels attend to all who do not get out of the way quickly enough. Now, drawn by stamping horses, comes the king's golden chariot.

Akhenaton stands as though lost in a dream and toys absent-mindedly with the small princesses, who have been allowed to ride along in the chariot and who amuse themselves by poking the horses from behind. Pharaoh hardly sees the populace around him. He is occupied with his own thoughts, for he is on his way to Aton's temple to pronounce the prayer for himself and for his people.

We follow in his wake toward the Temple of Aton. Over the street there is a bridge which links the king's private quarters with the official part of the palace. Around the royal residence there are double walls, and between them guards walk to and fro, watching over the king's divine person and over all those who enjoy the rare privilege of living in Pharaoh's own house.

We can only imagine the magnificence within—the great formal gardens, luxurious rooms with floors and walls decorated with frescoes that give the impression Nature itself has moved into the house. The walls seem to dissolve behind realistic paintings of stands of papyrus with birds soaring upward and calves dancing with joy in praise of Aton, the life-giving sun.

Then we reach the heart of the city—Aton's great temple. The high copper portals stand open, with halls of columns to the right and to the left. Akhenaton's image meets us everywhere, on small altarpieces and in large statues. We recognize them from the Aton temple in Amon's home in Karnak—the initial challenge which began the fight. But now they are no longer so extreme, so blasphemously exaggerated. In the new environment there is no longer any need to resort to such challenging forms.

Instead of the usual Egyptian temple, with its series of increasingly dark and secret-filled rooms, in which the closed, golden chapel of the god can barely be discerned in the darkness, this temple blinds us with light, which streams in from the open courts where offerings are made. Aton himself—he who is the warmth in the solar disk—fills the whole courtyard, and his rays shine down over countless altars, which overflow with offerings.

The king and queen have come forward to conduct the temple service. The hymn to Aton rises to the heavens, whose vaults of deep blue, sunlit infinity revolve, above the heads of all the worshipful listeners:

In beauty thou showest thyself at the heaven's eastern rim,
Thou, living Aton, creator of life.
Thou hast glowed forth in the East
And fillest all lands with thy beauty.
Beautiful art thou and great, shining high above the earth.
Thy rays encompass the nations—all that thou hast created.
Thou art far away, but thy rays are upon the earth,
All can see thee, but no man knows thy course

When thou goest down at the horizon in the West,
The world lies in darkness, as though in death.
The sleeping rest in their chambers, with heads covered over,
One eye cannot behold another.
The lion emerges from his lair,
The snake stings,
Darkness reigns,
The earth is silent . . .

Light envelops the earth, when thou risest on the horizon,
When thou shinest as Aton by day,
    and drivest away the darkness.
Thou sendest out thy rays
And the whole land is filled with rejoicing.
Men wake and rise up,
    for thou hast raised them . . .
Their arms are lifted in praise at thy dawning.

Cattle graze in contentment,
Trees and plants grow green,
Birds take flight from their nests,
Their wings praising thee.

All the animals gambol on their feet . . .
Fish in the streams dart before thee;

Thy rays penetrate the ocean depths . . .
Thou, who bringest harvests to men,
Who guardest the infant in his mother's womb,
Who comfortest him, until his tears cease . . .
Thou givest the breath of life to all which thou hast
    created . . .
When the birdling peeps in the egg,
Thou givest it air that it may live.

Manifold are thy works
Hidden from men.
Sole god, whose power is without equal,
Thou hast created the world after thine own heart,
    thou alone—
Men, beasts of every kind,
All that is on earth, that walks on feet,
All that is aloft, soaring on wings,
The foreign lands of Syria and Nubia
And Egypt's land.
Thou settest each man in his place
And createst all that he requires.
Each and every one has food
And the span of his life is measured.
Thou hast created the seasons of the year,
To fulfill all that thou hast brought forth.
Winter comes with coolness,
Summer's glow with thy heat.
Thou hast created the heavens, far from the earth,
To shine in them,
To behold from them,
All that thou hast created.

The hymn fades away—this wonderful creation which impressed even the enemies of Aton and which moves everyone by its deep religiosity, love, and humanity.

But outside the city, up against the desert mountains, we

see in the distance a large, square structure. The high walls rise up like fortifications, on which guards walk to and fro. Now and then we see soldiers patrolling the mountain heights behind them.

Does Akhenaton need fortifications and soldiers here in the capital city, in the heart of the country?

We approach the structure and find that this is the workers' quarter. For walls may serve just as well to confine people as to defend them from attackers. Enclosed by the walls lie small huts, all more or less the same, laid out in a military fashion in rows along narrow streets—exactly as in a concentration camp. Just inside the gates there is a large platform. There again we see an altarpiece with Akhenaton and Nefertiti beneath Aton's sun disk. Every morning the workers must line up to hail the ruler and his father, Aton, this god who supposedly supplies everyone's needs and dries everyone's tears.

But there is swelling discontent among the workers. This god's vaunted love and the hymn's words about Aton supplying all men's needs and drying their tears—all these seem bloodstained ironies. Hidden in dark crannies in the hovels are often small pictures of the old, tried gods, who had helped and comforted for thousands of years, who had healed the sick and given hope of eternal life after death—that death which Akhenaton's new teachings prefer not to mention.

One could turn to the old gods only in secret. Pharaoh had forbidden it. No gods were permitted to exist except for Aton. First he had seized Amon's goods and lands, disrupting the entire economic system. The finances of the land fell into disorder, but the true teaching was more important than anything else.

By the king's order howling mobs led by Akhenaton's followers had broken into thousand-year-old shrines, into graves and private houses, to destroy with religious fanaticism every trace of the hated name of Amon and, later, the names of all the other gods as well. Aton was to rule in solitary majesty.

At first, there were probably many who approved of curbing Amon's overweening power. But they soon grew frightened, even indignant over this extreme new intolerance toward all who thought differently. Its like had never been heard of, no matter how far back one searched in chronicles. Things had never taken this turn when Amon had forced aside the other gods, or when Re or Ptah or any other god had swung himself up to the highest rung in the divine hierarchy and so increased his earthly riches as well. Then one had said only that the new god was the greatest and mightiest of all the gods; the greater the others were, the greater was also the new god, to be first among them.

"How impractical Pharaoh is being! What a misfortune for the land! What riches are being squandered because of a royal whim!" Increasing numbers must have muttered words like these, as discontent burgeoned everywhere. Akhenaton had many enemies in the land, and he may well have needed to keep his troops in Egypt. But more than ever, Egypt needed troops outside its borders to defend the empire in Syria and Palestine. Akhenaton thought only of his god, not of his land and its vital interests.

To the north—in the interior of Asia Minor—the Hittite kingdom had grown into a major power, able to compete with Egypt. The princes of Syria covertly played along with the Hittites, who grew increasingly aggressive toward Egypt. City after city parted willingly from Egypt or was taken by force by Hittite allies. The whole Egyptian Empire in the north, created with so much blood and toil, was undergoing its death agonies.

From Byblos, a city on the Syrian coast with close ties to Egypt spanning more than a thousand years, a city already half Egyptian, there came constant pleas for help. After having faithfully fought for Pharaoh, the aged prince of Byblos, Ribaddi, had been driven from his city, and he now appeals to Akhenaton one last time:

"Ribaddi addresses his royal master, the sun of nations. At

Journal of Egyptian Archaeology

Head from a relief at El Amarna.

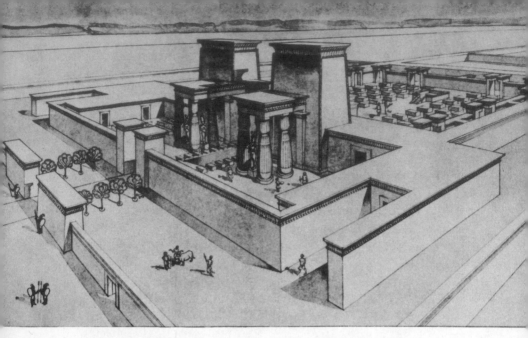

Journal of Egyptian Archaeology

Reconstruction of temple of Aton at El Amarna.

Model of Hatshepsut's temple at Deir el Bahri, reconstructed as it was in 480 B.C.

Metropolitan Museum of Art

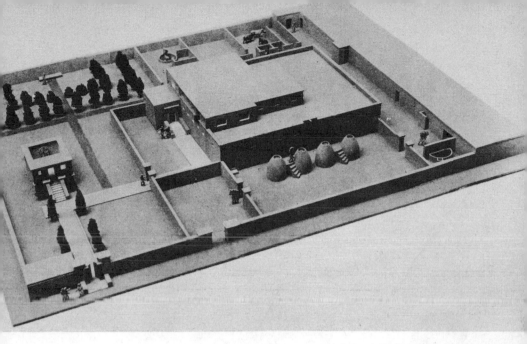

Journal of Egyptian Archaeology

Reconstruction of a rich man's house and living room
with couches and an altar to Aton, at El Amarna.

Journal of Egyptian Archaeology

Nefertiti.
Painted portrait bust from El Amarna. Berlin Museum.

the feet of my royal master, I bow down seven times seven times.

"I wrote repeatedly and asked for troops. But no troops were sent, and my master did not listen to the words of his servant. I sent my messenger to the royal court, but he returned with empty hands. No troops did he bring with him from Egypt. And my household saw this. When no silver came, they insulted me and the other princes, and showed contempt for me.

"Now I have traveled to Ammuniria, the prince of Beirut, and my younger brother has stirred up the city of Byblos in order to deliver it up to my master's enemies. When my brother saw that my messenger came back empty-handed and had no troops with him, then he scorned me and committed this crime and drove me from my city. May the king not remain inactive against this dog's misdeeds.

"See, I cannot journey to Egypt's lands. Two of my sons and my two wives have been handed over to the enemy. Myself, I am old, and my body is severely afflicted. May my royal master know that Byblos' gods are angry and that my pain is great.

"Therefore I cannot appear before my master's face, but my son, the king's servant, I have sent to my master. May the king now finally hear his servant's words and send soldiers, so that they and not the king's enemies may occupy Byblos. My royal master's soldiers have a burning desire to take possession of Byblos, and the day one hears of their arrival, the city of Byblos will go back to my master.

"May My Lord know that I die for him. When I am dead, my sons, so long as they live, will write to the king: 'Give us back our city!'

"Why has My Lord forsaken me?"

In Palestine, on the border of Egypt, the situation was just as bad. Desert bedouins—called the Chabiru—ravage the land, and Palestinian princes war among themselves. Abdi-Cheba, the king of Jerusalem, also tries to get Akhenaton to intervene and salvage the situation:

"To the king, My Lord, say I, Abdi-Cheba, your servant. At the feet of my royal master I bow down seven times seven times.

"So long as my royal master lives and so long as messengers travel, I shall say again and again: 'The king's lands are being laid waste.'

"But you do not listen to me.

"All the princes fall away—not a single prince will remain to my king. May the king turn his countenance toward the army, so that the soldiers may move into the field.

"None of the king's lands will remain. The Chabiru plunder all his lands.

"If the Egyptian troops come here this year, my royal master's lands will be retained. But if they do not come, my royal master's lands wil be lost.

"To my royal master's clerks says Abdi-Cheba, your servant: 'Put these words clearly before my royal master: All my royal master's lands are being laid waste!' "

But all the urgent entreaties and the desperate pleas for help are vain. The Egyptian occupation forces flee or are wiped out. Those who are loyal to the Egyptians are murdered or sold into slavery. Egyptian and Asian blood flows in torrents.

But Akhenaton is deaf to all pleas. He lets everything go as it will. The Egyptian army receives no order to march. Not because Akhenaton rejects on principle the use of armed force. Sometimes he sends a ridiculously inadequate troop contingent, and now and then he promises to send larger forces. But in Aton's horizon city the full extent of the danger is not perceived; the troops are needed in Egypt too. All attention is focused on one thing alone—Aton and his new teachings—and what can be done for them.

At last this could no longer be borne. Someone got Akhenaton to see that his position was untenable. Who it was, we do not know. Perhaps it was his mother, Queen Tiye, who earlier had once persuaded him to impress Aton's horizon city with his foreign policy by a public display—a parade in which tribute from all foreign lands was carried forward.

In any case, Akhenaton names his son-in-law, Semenchare, as co-regent and sends him to Thebes to negotiate a reconciliation with the priests of Amon.

But Queen Nefertiti does not understand the new policy. Heretofore, the two of them, Akhenaton and Nefertiti, had always lived in complete harmony. Portraits of them were everywhere displayed, depicting their domestic happiness. She had always been permitted to take an active part in state affairs and in the work of reform.

Now the idyll is shattered. King and queen go their separate ways; their households are completely divorced. Nefertiti takes with her the other son-in-law, Tutanchaton, and moves to a palace in the northern part of the horizon city. The king stays on in the southern palace, together with his son-in-law Semenchare.

In the northern palace they remove the names of Semenchare and his wife from all the inscriptions, to show that they will not hear of any reconciliation with Thebes and Amon.

The following year sees the deaths of both Semenchare and Akhenaton.

Akhenaton's final years must have been filled with infinite bitterness. All had failed. The great empire, Egypt's pride, lay shattered, and the enemy threatened Egypt's borders. His religious reform had never been understood. No one would or could see any advantage to worshiping one god, when there were several others, least of all a god who so badly protected the land and the empire against dangers. Akhenaton's elevated thoughts—his monotheism, if you will—came in the wrong place at the wrong time in world history. The new religion brought no one happiness, and thousands died for its sake. Their blood cried out to the heavens, but Aton could not help.

Tutanchaton now ascends the throne, and Nefertiti disappears—how or why, we do not know. Tutanchaton, a boy of eleven, moves back to Thebes, where he reconciles himself with Amon and changes his name from Tutanchaton to Tut-anchamon. As such he reigns for seven years, and when he dies at the age of eighteen, he is buried with pomp and splendor in the Valley of the Kings in Thebes, at the side of Egypt's rulers. His tomb would become world-famous because of the immense riches discovered there in the 1920s.

By an irony of fate this insignificant ruler, a puppet in the hands of Amon's priesthood and of the military, who wanted to re-establish the empire, became in our time the most famous name in Egyptian history. Great the restoration of Amon certainly was. The name of the king who reconciled himself with this god would live on men's lips across thousands of years.

But frenzied hatred was directed against Akhenaton and everything connected with him. Aton's horizon city was abandoned, and the desert reclaimed its soil. Aton's shrine was torn down; even its foundation stones were taken away. As though to purify a pest-ridden place, the foundation was covered over first with clean sand and then a layer of mortar. Akhenaton, who had called himself "child of the sun" and "the sun of nations," became for succeeding generations "the transgressor from Akhenaton," whose true name one did not want to utter.

Once again Amon had in triumph resumed his former place as "king of the gods," and the hymn in his honor rang out:

Woe to him who assails thee!
Thy city stands,
But the one which assailed thee was felled to the ground.
Woe to him who wrongs thee in any land!

He who knows thee not, Amon,
his sun goes down.
But he who knows thee,
over him the sun shines.

He who assailed thee,
his temple ground lies in darkness,

Although the whole earth streams with light.
He who clasps thee in his heart, Amon,
    see, his sun goes up.

Amon-Re, thou god of good fortune and abundance,
    who hath all life in thy care.
He who knows not thy name,
Woe to him to the end of his days.

King of Egypt and the Sudan

In Thebes there is a grave which belonged to a man named Huy. He was Pharaoh Tutanchamon's viceroy in the Egyptian colony in the northern Sudan, in the 1500s before Christ. He had his grave adorned with, among other things, a painting depicting himself in the exercise of his duties. Before Pharaoh's magnificent throne stands Huy, receiving taxpayers from Nubia and the Sudan. They have heaped up mounds of gold and other raw materials such as ostrich plumes and panther skins. They have also brought a set of beautiful furniture and other products of craftsmanship in pure Egyptian style.

At the head of the delegation kneel the Nubian princes. Although they are dressed in fine Egyptian court costumes of thin linen, their outfits must have given the Egyptians much the same impression that we get from the sight of an African chief wearing a top hat with his native dress. For over their court costumes the Nubians wear brightly colored bands and panther skins, and they have feathers in their hair—adornments which would all be most unsuitable for an Egyptian official.

Last in the procession comes a chariot drawn by oxen and in the chariot a Nubian princess. No doubt she is destined for Pharaoh's harem. She, too, wears an Egyptian linen costume and is adorned with Egyptian jewelry. Like all fine ladies of the time, she is protected from the burning rays of the sun by a large fan made of ostrich plumes. In her case, however, the purpose of the fan can hardly be to ward off an unflattering sunburn, its purpose for her Egyptian colleagues, for the natural color of her skin is just as dark as that of her Negro companions.

The chariot in which she rides is not just any old oxcart, but a slender and light construction of rare woods. There is only one thing wrong with it; it was not at all intended to be drawn by gentle oxen. It is a light battle chariot, of the type used by the Egyptian chariot warriors when they established the great Egyptian empire from the heart of the Sudan in the south to the Euphrates in the north. Such a chariot should really, of course, have been drawn by fiery stallions. The Egyptians must have regarded this much as we would regard a Rolls-Royce hitched to plow horses.

The title and the name of one of the Nubian chiefs have also been immortalized here. He is "prince of Miam," and he bears the Egyptian name "Hekanefer," which means "the good prince." By pure coincidence, we know a little about this man. Miam was an Egyptian administrative center in northern Nubia—in our day the place is called Aniba—and not far from here is an inscription on a cliff which mentions this same Hekanefer. There he has a title which shows that he had received a good education at the Egyptian court. Anyone who had received this kind of training was permitted to adopt a special title, and whether he was foreign or Egyptian, he delighted in bearing this honorary title to the day he died, no matter what station he later attained in society.

This tomb painting, with all its picturesque details, gives us a good idea of the ancient Egyptian colonial policy in the Sudan during its heyday in the latter half of the second millennium before Christ.

When, as sometimes happens in today's discussions about the Sudan, the Egyptian side offers historical reasons in further support of a union of Egypt and the Sudan, this period is probably the one which they can invoke most effectively. Some ten years ago, when I wrote a dissertation on the ancient Egyptian colonial policy in the south, I had no idea that these ancient problems could ever acquire a current political significance. But the fact is that the Egypt of today has taken an extraordinary interest lately in precisely this historical aspect, which, for example, was one of the arguments for the title "king of Egypt and the Sudan" which King Farouk assumed. The aspirations implied in this title seem not at all to have disappeared with the fall of the monarchy and the advent of the republic. If we make allowances for the conditions of the time and do not set too high requirements, we can also give a rather good grade to the colonial policy of ancient Egypt. It is due to this, no doubt, that the policy can still have a certain value as propaganda, even today.

In earlier times the Egyptians had first tried to solve their colonial problems in the south through quite different methods. What they were after was not a region in which to locate their surplus population. Egypt did not then suffer from overpopulation, as it does today. What interested the Pharaohs were the Sudan's rich natural resources. At first, during the time of the pyramids, they had been able to tap these raw materials without any reaction on the part of the native population. But this good relationship was broken off when powerful new tribes wandered into the southern Sudan. In the regions between the first and second cataracts of the Nile, the Nubians hampered Egyptian trade in every possible way. After diverse raids, the Egyptians decided, in the 1950s before Christ, to conquer and to occupy militarily the whole northern part of the region closest to the Egyptian border, a region which also in our own time belongs to Egypt politically, but hardly at all culturally.

In order to manage the proud, self-respecting Nubians, the Egyptians instituted a harsh military regime. The Nubian chiefs were forced to wash for gold for the Egyptians, and the people were treated as slaves. This policy of force naturally provoked a reaction among the natives. In order to hold the region the Egyptians had to build strong fortresses both in the Nubian population centers and near the gold mines. The political relationship which prevailed between ruler and subject was very tense. "If you attack him, he falls back, but if you yourself fall back, he attacks," says an Egyptian king about his Nubian opponent in this era. A wealth of archeological sources tell us that the Nubians would not permit a single purely Egyptian object to be placed in their graves, but remained stubbornly loyal to what was theirs alone.

South of the occupied territory, down in the regions of the third Nile cataract, the Egyptians succeeded, conversely, in bringing about peaceful trade relations which benefited both sides. Here the graves of natives contained so many Egyptian luxury goods that the men who first uncovered them believed them to be Egyptian graves.

Around 1600 B.C. wars broke out in Egypt between Asians, who had made themselves masters of the land, and their Egyptian provincial governors. Now, when no one had time any longer to hold them in check, the Nubians seized their opportunity to throw off the hated foreign yoke. Then we see an interesting development. The Nubians, who had rejected the higher culture of their Egyptian masters so long as they were kept in subjection, become in a very short time—perhaps only one generation—so firmly Egyptianized that the indigenous culture loses all its inner force. At one blow the aversion to Egypt disappears and Nubian soldiers even help the Egyptians drive the Asian foreigners from Egyptian soil.

But ingratitude is the world's wage, and as soon as Egypt had once again become a strong, united nation, the Egyptians moved against their Nubian allies' homeland. Now they were not content to conquer only the northern part, nearest to Egypt. The Egyptian troops finally halted more than five hundred miles south of Egypt where the fourth cataract of the Nile, with its almost impassable falls, forms a natural barrier. On a few occasions they advanced even farther.

The Egyptians now changed their tactics in the conquered territory. Before, they had tried to control the natives by military force, but now they did everything to win them to their side. Culturally they succeeded very quickly, since Egyptianization was far advanced even before the conquest. At times their use of the blessings of Egyptian culture may have been a bit eccentric, as we saw in the tomb painting, but the process in any case went so far that archeologists of today cannot distinguish between Egyptian and Nubian graves in the region. And the products of handicraft in the colony were fine enough to satisfy Egyptian taste and to serve as currency for paying taxes to Pharaoh.

In principle the administration of the colony was similar to that of a British colony in our own times. A very small number of Egyptian officials were stationed there, under the leadership of a viceroy, and for the more difficult tasks specialists were sent out. The purely Egyptian participation in the administrative apparatus was certainly very small numerically. To the Egyptians, there was something uninviting about living in any place other than their homeland. Aside from those who were stationed there under orders or who were sent there as convicts, there were certainly no Egyptians who moved to the Sudanese province. Indicative of this is an inscription found on the door of the home of an Egyptian official living in Nubia: "When you enter this house, may you think yourself in Thebes [the Egyptian capital] and rejoice." This strong love for the homeland, expressed in these texts and always an Egyptian characteristic, certainly helped produce the policy of allowing the Nubians to manage themselves to the greatest degree practicable.

The normal routine work was turned over to the more or less Egyptianized petty kings of Nubia. As early as this time, over three thousand years ago, the Egyptians anticipated the British policy of encouraging colonial princes to be educated in home country schools and universities. The sons of the Nubian petty monarchs were taken to Egypt and placed at court, where they were brought up with the Egyptian princes and sons of the higher officials. In this way they became still more Egyptianized, and it is very possible that they also came to be more loyal to their Egyptian colleagues, with whom they had grown up, than to the Nubians, whom they never met during their formative years.

Not all of the Nubians educated in Egypt returned to their homeland, for some of them stayed on in Egypt. To be sure, there was a certain prejudice against foreigners in ancient Egypt, but there were no legal obstacles to prevent them from rising in society. A Nubian, for example, could perfectly well be the heir of an Egyptian court barber, who leaves his "shop" as a legacy to a prisoner of war whom he had acquired in the course of a campaign. In general it was in just this role of a personal servant to the king, or to some highly placed Egyptian, that the Nubian could achieve a good station in life and even a very high official post.

During this period Nubia and the northern Sudan were flourishing—with peaceful and orderly conditions prevailing generally throughout the colony. Great riches flowed into Egypt, but the general well-being of the inhabitants was also rising. A state of affairs had been attained with which both sides could be content and in which the Nubians stood loyally at the side of their Egyptian rulers.

The final chapter in the ancient Egyptian policy toward the Sudan came a couple of hundred years later. This is a chapter

G. Eriksson

Princess. From El Amarna.

Presentation of Nubian tribute to Pharaoh.
Wall painting from Thebes. Fourteenth century B.C.

which has less value as propaganda from the Egyptian view-
point but which, conversely, the Sudanese may be quite pleased
to recall.

In the 700s B.C. the Egyptian state had entered upon a period
of political weakness. Even earlier the Nubian region and the
northern Sudan had freed themselves from Egypt. Now, instead, it is the Sudanese who intervene in Egyptian internal
politics. From the city of Napata, all the way down by the
fourth cataract, Sudanese rulers moved northward, gained a
foothold in the old capital of Thebes, and then conquered the
whole land up to the Delta in the north.

But as a natural result of the Egyptian method of colonization, these dark-skinned conquerors from the Sudan acted not
at all like foreign barbarians. They regarded themselves as the
true champions of the ancient Egyptian religion and culture.
Wherever they marched in Egypt the Sudanese worshiped the
Egyptian gods, observing the time-honored rites in which they
had been versed during Egyptian colonization. In the eyes of
the Sudanese, the Egyptians of the north were degenerate de-
scendants of a proud past. The first conqueror from the Sudan
did not permit the Delta princes to enter his house because,
as it says in the victory inscription, "They were unclean and
fisheaters, which of course is something detestable"—according
to ancient Egyptian religious laws, in any case.

It is during this time of the Sudanese rulers that the so-called
Egyptian renaissance begins, when the attempt is made in art
and literature to revive the old ideals from Egypt's more classic
ages, when its culture was the highest in the Near East. And
it is these foreigners who succeed, for a time, in defending their
former Egyptian masters against the terrible onslaughts of the
Assyrians in the 600s.

When at last they had to flee from the field of battle, they
drew back to the Sudan once again. Even then, their flowering kingdom in the south, inheritor of the ancient Egyptian
culture in the Sudan, appears to Greek writers of history as a

legendary land where men are more happy and long-lived than anywhere else.

In so far as the element of Egyptian culture contributed to this evolution of the Sudan, we may surely regard this, too, as a good recommendation for the Egyptian colonial policy in the south.

The solitary victor

In the year 1285 B.C., Pharaoh Ramses II made camp near
the city of Kadesh, in Syria. This was one of the strongest
fortresses in all Syria. It lay in a region which had long been
fought over by the two great powers of the time, Egypt and
the Hittite nation. Sometimes it belonged to one side, sometimes to the other. Ramses II was making a massive effort to
solve the problem definitively.

On the march north the Egyptians had captured some Hittite
deserters who assured them that the Hittite king, Muwatallis,
and the entire Hittite army were far away up in northern Syria,
in the vicinity of the city of Aleppo. Ramses II had believed
their reports and had permitted the Egyptian forces to move
forward in extended-march order. Now when he made his
halt at Kadesh with the first section, the so-called Amon's

Division, the closest Egyptian strength was still on the march more than a mile to the south, and the rest of the Egyptian forces were nine miles farther away.

In this situation, with the Egyptian army spread out over a large area and least ready to do battle, Ramses II learned the terrible truth. The captured Hittite deserters had actually been sent out by King Muwatallis to deceive the Egyptians. Muwatallis himself, with the whole Hittite army, was just on the other side of the hill on which Kadesh was situated and where Ramses and his lead troops had made camp.

Now the Hittites took the offensive. Ramses and his Amon's Division managed to repulse the initial attack on the Egyptian camp; but in the meantime another Hittite troop had routed Egyptian forces still on the march. When these forces, in panic, came fleeing north to the camp they drew the Amon's Division with them in flight. They all fled in wild terror and left Ramses II in the lurch. Pharaoh was surrounded by 2500 Hittite chariots, or 7500 warriors, since there were three men on each chariot.

Ramses himself recounts that he was "completely alone." "No officer was with me, no driver, no non-commissioned officer, and my infantry and my chariot forces were easy marks for the Hittites, since no one made a stand and fought them."

In this moment of despair he offered up a prayer to his father, the god Amon, in the firm knowledge that "Amon was worth more to him than millions of infantrymen, chariots by the hundreds of thousands, tens of thousands of brothers and sons even if they stood wholeheartedly united," which, of course, they had fatally not done in this perilous situation. Strengthened by his prayer, he went alone to the attack. "Not one of the enemy was able to fight, for their hearts trembled with terror of me," says Ramses. "Their weapons were powerless, so that they could neither hurl nor find courage to take up their lances. I made them splash down in the water like crocodiles . . . and I killed those I felt like killing."

Now that Ramses, if we may trust his own words, had won

a decisive victory, auxiliary troops appeared on the battlefield. With their help the Egyptians retook their camp, which the Hittites had overrun and were now plundering of all the costly items which, despite the hardships of a campaign, an Egyptian Pharaoh took along in the field to maintain a suitable establishment. Then another Egyptian division arrived, and, according to Egyptian accounts, this battle which had begun so inauspiciously turned into a crushing defeat for the Hittites.

After the battle Ramses reviewed his troops and upbraided them for having abandoned him and left him to fight alone against the 2500 Hittite chariots, without even daring to look on as he, the king, achieved the victory all by himself. When you read the Egyptian account, you almost wonder why Ramses really bothered to bring along an entire army, when he could finish off the war just as well without it.

This personal victory of Ramses II was glorified in practically all the large temples Ramses built in Egypt and in the Nubian province to the south. On the great gate-towers, the pylons, the battle was depicted in colossal reliefs. We see Ramses, surrounded by the enemy chariots, driving the Hittites into the Orontes River. Hittite men and princes are swimming to escape to the other side of the river, where their fellow soldiers are fishing them out. On one such relief we see the Hittite king's own son swimming along with feeble strokes. Another prince has reached shore, where his soldiers turn him upside down to empty out the water.

It is probably due largely to these gigantic temple buildings and the handsome, monumental depictions of his unique victory at Kadesh that Ramses II has become the best known, perhaps, of the Egyptian Pharaohs. This is not wholly deserved, surely, since many of his temples were simply taken over from earlier kings who had built the main sections.

What about this great victory, anyway?

Hittite sources give us more the impression that the battle was an Egyptian defeat and that, far from having succeeded in crushing the Hittite army, Ramses was forced after the battle to withdraw quickly to the south, to avoid having his route of retreat cut off. The Hittites marched south along the more convenient coastal route in order to hinder Ramses II's retreat. Ramses had to wend his way back through less easily traveled regions in the interior. That the battle, presented as a great victory, was actually a strategic fiasco, cannot be doubted.

How then can we explain why this event should be used by Ramses as his main propaganda turn, and how can the story of the king who defeats 7500 enemies all by himself, which seems quite laughable to us, ever have had any other effect than to provoke ridicule and skepticism?

To understand this we must look a bit closer at the religious and political background. It often happens that something which seems inexplicable and even ridiculous to the outsider can be explained quite naturally, once a clear conception is acquired of the context and historical background of the event. After all, it is sometimes said that if Hitler had appeared in another country at another time, from the first moment he would have been rendered harmless by hearty laughter. That he was able to seize power is surely due in part to the very fact that those who lived in another environment and another political atmosphere refused for some time to take seriously this phenomenon, often so ridiculous in its outward forms.

The motif of the king who conquers the enemy singlehandedly was not something new launched by Ramses. The Egyptians had heard it before without reacting as we might have expected. Two centuries earlier the warrior king Amenophis II proclaimed that, alone on the battlefield, and dependent only on his own sword, he had crushed the enemy's army. The same story was told of his father, Tuthmosis III, who established the Egyptian empire in Syria and Palestine. Because such a small percentage of official victory proclamations and similar texts have come down to us, pure chance guides us in tracing how often and under which kings this theme of the solitary victor reappeared. It was probably far more common than we might suspect from the texts which have been preserved. This we can infer from the fact that we also find this theme, in an isolated instance, under Sesostris III, the king who conquered the Nubian region south of Egypt six hundred years before Ramses and who again was one of Egypt's great warrior kings. A hymn to Sesostris tells us that he was "the youthful solitary one, who fights for his border."

The conception of the king as "the solitary, the sole" is not only limited to the battlefield. Quite often the king's residence is called "the palace of the solitary one" or "the solitary one's dwelling," and in the time of the pyramids, twelve hundred years before Ramses, when the burial hymn was sung over the dead king, he was once again called "the solitary, sole." At this time the king was identified with the highest god, as he was not in later times, and I think it is in this identity that we must seek the explanation and background of both the term "the solitary one" and the account of the victory at Kadesh, which we find so curious.

As is often the case with something we find inexplicable and contrary to sense, it is on the religious plane that we can find the explanation, perhaps just as "unreasonable" but in any case natural and comprehensible in psychological terms.

In the Egyptian account of the battle at Kadesh, there is one detail which indicates where we should seek our explanation. One of the Hittites who is assaulted by Ramses, shouts to his comrades:

"This is no man who is among us, but [the god] Sutech, great in strength, and [the god] Baal himself! No man has ever done so great a deed as he is performing. Has a man ever slain hundreds of thousands, without having any infantry or any chariots fighting on his side? Let us flee from him and try to save our lives!"

When Ramses crushes the enemy, he is not an ordinary man. He is performing as a god. "His strength is that of the war god Monthus, his appearance as beautiful as [the creator god] Atum's," we hear from another source.

To the Egyptians, Pharaoh was never a man; he was a god

on earth. We have no reason to doubt that this was really a living, self-evident article of faith for the Egyptians. If you think of the roles which a Mussolini, a Hitler, and a Stalin have played in modern times, when religion and religious thought, although very different, have been pushed into the background, you can at least imagine the atmosphere from which this faith sprang up.

If we succeed in understanding what Pharaoh's divinity really implies, the almost ridiculous story of the solitary victor will no longer seem so strange. This is particularly true, if we consider what role the theme of "the solitary one," "the sole one," played in religion and theology.

Before the creation of the ordered world reigned chaos, an undifferentiated ocean, called Nun. Then a small hill rose above the water, a firm spot on which the creator and god takes his stance and creates the cosmos, the ordered world. When the god does this, he is "the solitary sole one," as he must be logically, since, according to Egyptian belief, he was the first and eldest of the gods, who existed when nothing else did and nothing else had taken form. As one text puts it, he is "the sole one [the solitary] who made what is and created the existing, who joined together the limbs of creatures, a living torch of light which rose from [the waters of chaos] Nun."

To the Egyptians, the creation of the ordered world, the cosmos, was the only really significant event in history. All that happened later during centuries and millenniums, the conflicts in internal and foreign politics, had no great importance. These simply meant that the powers of chaos had achieved a minor disturbance of the cosmos, and if you believed in the religion at all, you were firmly convinced that soon everything would be put right again through the intervention of the gods. Each such intervention implied a repetition of the first act of creation. This constant re-creation of the cosmos by the creator god was the essence of the Egyptians' religious faith and, in the literal sense, an everyday miracle.

The god driving away the powers of darkness was the main

Journal of Egyptian Archaeology

"May you think yourself in Thebes, and rejoice."
Egyptian official and Nubians.
Relief from the tomb of Haremheb, fourteenth century B.C.

Fallen colossus of Ramses II, Thebes. Thirteenth century B.C.

Fragment of a yellow jasper head of Queen Teyz.

Ramses III hunting wild bulls.
Colossal relief at Medinet Habu. Twelfth century B.C.

theme in daily worship in the temples. Corresponding to the Christian Easter, this victory over evil and the enemies of the gods culminated in the New Year celebrations, following the last five days of the year, when the demons had threatened to take the upper hand. In the rites of this cult the king often played the role of the god who conquered the evil powers. Since the country's enemies and the evil powers of chaos were one and the same to the Egyptians, it was natural that every victory over a foreign enemy should be regarded as a creator god's victory over the power of chaos. As in the temple ceremonies, the king thereby performed a holy rite, in which he had the role of the creator god, the highest of the gods.

Against this background, what seems to us a ridiculous exaggeration, the king as solitary victor, does not appear to be solely—or even primarily, I think—a propaganda device for the king. It seems to be rather a statement of religious faith, a hymn to the divine power and its ability constantly to re-create the cosmos, the ordered world, even when it looks as though the powers of chaos, the enemies of Egypt and the king, are going to win out entirely.

But this equation—yes, even identification—of the king with the creator god is simply one aspect of the relationship between Pharaoh and the highest god, and it gives us only a partial background to the Kadesh story. As solitary warrior and victor, Ramses is identified with the highest god, with the one who can crush the power of chaos, the enemy. How then can we explain why Ramses at this crucial moment prays to his father Amon, the highest god, and in moving words, asks him for help.

"What is this now, O my father Amon? Has ever a father forgotten his son, or is this then something which I have done against thy will?" The words "My God, my God, why hast thou forsaken me?" come unbidden to mind.

This prayer, this dependence on the highest god, seems to be in direct contrast to the role which the king plays when, as the creator god, he conquers the enemy and restores, re-creates, the ordered world. To us this seems a logical somersault.

But Egyptian religious logic is not the same as ours. Such incompatible beliefs and conflicting explanations, which strike us as totally confused and confusing, never bothered the believing Egyptian. We encounter them constantly in Egyptian religion.

This duality, in which the king can act simultaneously as the highest creator god and as the god's dependent son, has its explanation in the historical development of the ideology of kingship through centuries and millenniums.

Behind this duality lies a split between two completely different conceptions of the king: an older one, according to which the king is the highest god; a later one, according to which he is the son of the highest god and his divine representative on earth. This split, and the oscillations between the divine king and the highest god, can be traced throughout Egyptian history. Behind it can be discerned a power struggle between the king and the priesthood . . . between church and state, if you will. From this fascinating interplay, involving both power politics and the evolution of basic beliefs, stems much of what is most essential and universally appealing in the ancient Egyptian culture. A typical product of this interplay is this very account of Ramses II's victory, which we find so peculiar.

Ramses III, the last great Pharaoh

In the 1200s before Christ the catastrophe came. For some reason barbarian tribes in the Danube region began to rouse themselves. Some moved down in plundering bands toward Greece, where the Mycenaean culture flourished. City after city, town after town fell to the invaders; but the chief city, the storied Mycenae, managed to hold out. The folk wave moved on over Crete and southwestern Asia Minor and then to the North African coast, where the tribes combined with the Libyans to attack Egypt. The invasion was thrown back, but this was only the first warning.

Another tribe, the Phrygians, rolled in over Asia Minor from the Danube region. The Hittite kingdom, which had not long before been one of the strongest military powers in the Middle East, was shattered and annihilated. After about 1200 B.C. historical sources are silent about this realm.

The pressure of the ravaging migrations only increased.

Tribes from Greece in the west and Asia Minor in the north gathered in northern Syria for the final assault upon the richest and most tempting region in the eastern Meditterranean world, the fertile Nile Delta of Egypt.

What was the situation in Egypt in this hour of peril? After the attack by the Libyans and the new peoples from the north, the country had known hard times. If we may believe Ramses III's account: "The land was cast end over end. For several years there was no supreme ruler . . . and Egypt lay in the hands of great men and city princes. Each one killed the other, both great and small. Other times came after many empty years [without rulers], and a Syrian, Irsu, made himself ruler among them. He put the whole land under obligation to pay him taxes, collected about him men like himself, and plundered [the Egyptians] of all their possessions. The gods were treated like ordinary men, and no offerings were made in their temples.

"But when the gods again became merciful . . . they established their son, he who had issued from their limbs, as ruler over the whole land . . . he, Sethnacht, beloved of Re and Amon. . . . He re-established order in the land which had been in revolt, and he killed those who caused unrest.

"He made me the crown prince. I became the highest official in Egypt's lands and the one who governed the whole country.

"When he went to his rest on the horizon . . . I was crowned the Amon-Re, master of the gods Re-Atum, and Ptah of the beautiful face as master over both the lands."

Since Ramses III's father, Sethnacht, who appears here as a savior in a time of need, was a usurper with no legal right to the throne, it is very likely that the internal political situation is pictured here in rather too dark colors, for the propagandistic purpose of justifying the usurpation. We know, for example, that two of the land's highest officials held the same posts before, during, and after the period which Ramses depicts as a time of absolute political decay, and this fact among others indicates that the anarchy can hardly have been quite so complete.

But in the case of external politics there is no doubt that

danger was imminent. What had quickly to be done was to collect the land's scattered forces and carry out an effective preparedness program. Hundreds of thousands, both Egyptians and foreign mercenaries, were enrolled in the infantry and the chariot forces, Ramses III tells us.

This was at the last minute. Now the assaults came, one after another, first from Libya to the northwest. To pacify this region, Ramses had tried to put in a Libyan prince raised in Egypt as king of Libya. The attempt failed, and the Libyan tribes, in one combined force, broke into the Delta in northern Egypt. But before they had time to reach the heart of the land, Ramses managed to inflict a stinging defeat, and they were forced to retreat.

In the meantime, up in the northeastern corner of the Mediterranean, where the coasts of Asia Minor and Syria meet, the threat was growing.

"The foreign nations," we are told, "had conspired together on their islands. All lands were annihilated and crushed [by them]. No land could hold out against their weapons, neither the Hittite land, Kode, Carcemish, Cilicia, nor Cyprus. All were annihilated. They made camp in one place in the land of the Amorites and plundered its people, and the land looked as though it had never existed. And now they neared Egypt."

These were the so-called "peoples of the sea"—the Peleset (which is to say the Philistines), the Thekel, the Danai, and others who had formed a terrifying coalition. One group moved by oxcart, like a swarm of lemmings, along the coast through Syria and Palestine. Another group steered their slender sailing ships toward the mouths of the Nile. The time was long past when the Egyptian fleet controlled the ocean, and there was no possibility of countering the enemy sea power along the way. But Ramses III made a virtue of necessity and permitted them to enter the narrow Nile channels unopposed. There the trap was sprung, like a birdcatcher permitting a flock of ducks to settle on his net only to close it about them at the right moment.

The ships of the sea people, under full sail, had barely veered into the Nile when they were showered with well-aimed arrows and spears from the Egyptian infantry drawn up along the shores. Before the enemy had time to recover, Egyptian river boats swarmed around the fleet. The sea peoples' ships had no oars, and they were speedily outmaneuvered by the more easily guided, rowed vessels of the Egyptians. The Egyptians boarded the enemy ships, seized the ropes of their sails, and forced them to capsize. The catastrophe for the enemy was total.

"All those who reached my borders, their seed no longer exists; their hearts and souls are annihilated for eternity. They who came by sea, a flaming fire met them, a barrier of lances surrounded them on the shore; they were pulled to shore like parcels, heaved up on land, killed and thrown in piles," Ramses III exults.

The sea peoples' assault by land also failed, and they were forced to retreat north. The Peleset, the Philistines, settled in Palestine. Their allies, the Danai, we find later in southern Turkey, near the Syrian border; the others met unknown fates.

The triumph was complete. At the last moment Ramses had succeeded in saving Egypt from the terrible fate which had befallen all the other lands, large and small, in the western part of the Near East. There the old states had been splintered as though by an atom bomb, and nameless suffering was the people's lot in this witches' brew of migrating tribes.

Egypt was saved, but still no rest was possible. A new ruler in Libya, named Kaper, had once again united all the Libyan tribes for an attack on Egypt. Under the leadership of Kaper's son Mesher the Libyan forces had soon advanced deep into the land. But once more Ramses succeeded in winning a glowing victory. Among the numerous prisoners was also the Libyan prince and army chief, Mesher. His aged father pleaded for his son's life. But in vain. The son was killed, and the father dragged off into slavery.

The Libyans in general were too valuable as warriors simply to be slaughtered in honor of Amon, the god of their realm. They were put in prison camps, where "they may hear the speech of people in the retinue of the king," as the Egyptians put it, "and he saw to it that their own language disappeared and that they forgot their own tongue." After this re-education they were enrolled in the Egyptian army.

Now began a golden age in Egyptian history. The tax system was reorganized, and riches in never-ending supply flowed into the state treasury. In all directions expeditions were sent out to procure precious raw materials—gold from the south, copper from the Sinai, incense and myrrh from Somaliland. Enormous temples were built to the gods, these gods who had been so badly treated but who had given Ramses glowing victories and rescued the land in its hour of danger. The temples, filled with gold and silver, precious stones, and mounds of grain and other foods, were decorated with brightly painted reliefs, not a few of them pictures of the king's shining exploits in war.

These works of art have colossal dimensions, but at the same time they also achieve a truly monumental style. In some of these works the Egyptian artists outdo themselves and achieve brilliant creations in a genre in which they had never before attained such a unified effect.

Not only the king and the gods enjoyed the fruits of the victories and the work of reconstruction. At least, not if we may believe Ramses III: "Throughout the whole land, I planted trees and greenery and let the people sit in their shade. I made it so that a woman in Egypt might go wherever she willed without anyone accosting her on the way." Both Egyptian soldiers and foreign mercenaries could stretch out on their backs, since there were no longer any enemies to fight, neither in Nubia nor in Syria. "Their bows and weapons lay in the storehouses, and they were sated and full of happiness with their wives and children, who were with them. I supported all in the land, both foreigners and Egyptians, both men and women."

Ramses emphasizes particularly that the administration of justice functioned so well that even the less important man could maintain his rights against his superior.

It sounds almost too good to be true. If we look at the monuments which have been preserved, at the handsome buildings, the riches in the hands of the state and the priesthood, it seems like a Utopia. This state splendor and the flowery phrases of the official texts were meant to bear witness to posterity of Ramses III's fortunate reign. If pure chance had not preserved for us some insignificant papyri and inscribed pottery fragments, we should almost have taken him at his word. But when we read these everyday documents, the picture becomes quite different—a fascinating contrast to the glossy exterior.

In Thebes a rather large group of families specialized in the pious work of digging and painting handsomely the royal tombs in the Valley of the Kings in the desert mountains west of Thebes. Their small city, Deir el Medineh, as it is now called, has been closely studied by archeologists, who have found a large number of texts and other materials which give us an insight into the life and times of these workers. There are artists' sketches and writing exercises, pictures of the wear and tear of everyday life, of the sources of joy and dissension. In a controversy over the right to a family burial plot it is apparent that too much confidence was placed in Ramses' vaunted justice, since they prefer to turn to divine oracles rather than to the earthly judges. It was cheaper, and the chance of obtaining justice was about equally great.

Among these often quite trivial things we also find something more worthy of attention—the earliest testimony regarding strikes by workers.

It begins with an inscription on a little pottery fragment, which tells us that on the twenty-first day in the second month of the twenty-ninth year of Ramses III's reign, the clerk Amennacht said to the workers: "Now twenty days of the month have passed, and we have still not received our rations." So he went to a temple in the vicinity and there managed to obtain a portion of their pay. This first time it seems to have been possible to pacify the workers by borrowing from temple stores in the region. Properly, it was the state treasury and not the temples which should have paid the workers.

But then come more difficulties, so severe that Amennacht thought it best to keep a record of them, which has been preserved. On the twenty-ninth day of the seventh month the workers in the Valley of the Kings stop their work and make their way past the five guard walls at the entrance to the valley. The work on the royal grave was watched over carefully, and guards were necessary to protect the unbelievable riches which had been placed in the graves of earlier kings.

The workers march down to the large temples in the Nile Valley and institute a sit-down strike. One night is passed in great disorder in Ramses II's temple, the Ramesseum, and neither fair means nor foul can get them back to work.

"We are hungry," they shout. "Hunger and thirst have driven us here. We have no clothes, no oil, no fish, no vegetables! Send a message to Pharaoh, our master, or the vizier, our chief, so that we may receive something to survive on!"

Only after several days of disturbances are the rations for the previous month paid out to them, and the workers content themselves with this—for a while. Next month is just as bad, and the month following the vizier himself has to appear before them to calm them. Not even he can pay them in full, but by his authority he manages to make them accept half their pay. The administrative apparatus no longer functions as it should. The vizier tells them frankly, but also indignantly: "Have I not given you as much as all the other viziers? And if it should now happen that nothing is left in the grain supply, I have given you what I could find [from other sources]."

It was apparently common for the workers in the necropolis, who still were among the most privileged workers in the land, to have to wait long, and often in vain, for their pay. Even the vizier himself, like his subordinates, had to go out and borrow in order to make the salary payments.

The workers sometimes tried to sustain themselves in other ways. One of them was charged with having taken stone from the grave of Ramses II—perhaps a quiet attempt to have the late king pay his arrears with some of his rich burial accoutrements. The same man went and stole an ox from one of the temples. That he moreover led astray three of his colleagues' wives may be less excusable.

In such circumstances it is no wonder that Ramses III had to begin looking after his own house. Around his luxurious temple in Thebes and the adjoining palace he built a strong fortified wall, with battlements and towers, to safeguard the temple treasures from disorderly elements. A large fortification in the very heart of the land—a defense against the land's own people—made a striking image of the beginning dissolution.

If we look more closely at this structure, we find other features which indicate that Ramses III's life, despite the outward splendor and the handsome phrases, was not a bed of roses. In the largest gate tower in the fortification wall we find pictures of the king surrounded by a crowd of charming harem women. And in his palace within the temple walls lies a series of rooms for the harem women, just in back of the king's grand audience chamber. These harem rooms are all exactly like one another, as though Ramses had wanted not to show his particular favor to any of his consorts, to avoid all nagging and envy among the wives.

The same impartiality reigns in the pictures. A few wives occupy more prominent positions than the others, but the names are never inscribed on any of their portraits. Thus any one of the women in the harem might identify herself with the lady particularly privileged.

More was at stake here than simply keeping peace among the wives. It was a question of who among all the sons of his wives should be the successor to the throne. This would be that prince whose mother had been designated as the favorite, "The great royal consort." This was a vital affair of state, not a question of peace in the family.

For as long as possible Ramses postponed this choice, as though he foresaw its consequences. But not even the divine Pharaoh could hope to live forever here on earth. Finally he had to decide, but when he did, frightful turmoil was the

View of the valley of the Kings, Thebes.

Head of ibis from figure of Thoth.

result. In the tangle of intrigues and counterintrigues, Ramses III himself was murdered, and as victor among the candidates stood his successor on the throne, Ramses IV.

We have good reason to believe that he was not the one whom Ramses III had chosen as crown prince; the later kings regarded Ramses IV as a usurper without legitimate right to the throne. Ramses IV did what he could to cleanse himself and to justify his role in the terrible blood bath among his opponents. Among other things, he issued an account of their trial which has been preserved down to our own day.

According to this text, Ramses III himself, before his death, is supposed to have set up judges to punish the guilty, whoever they might be—but only after close scrutiny, so that no one innocent should be made to suffer.

Among those most seriously charged is Prince Pentawer, probably the one whom Ramses III had chosen as crown prince. He is accused of having placed himself on his mother's side when she, together with other harem women, conspired and tried to stir up the people against their lord. "They found him guilty; they left him where he was; he took his own life," the record tells us.

A number of higher officials, among them an officer and a police captain, are accused of having been in collusion with some women who had sneaked away from the harem, and even of having a beer party with the women, instead of reporting them. Their terrible punishment was to have their noses and ears cut off. One of them committed suicide after undergoing this torture.

Numerous officials and others fell victims to the stern judgments. The normal punishment was death. That this was more than the usual harem intrigue common in the Orient is obvious. Not only harem officials were involved, but also representatives of the police power and of the troops in Egypt and in the rich Nubian province to the south. Civil war threatened until Ramses IV managed to usurp power before the other side had time to strike.

Egypt seems never to have recovered from this internal crisis, of which the worker strikes and the harem conspiracy were symptomatic. After the death of Ramses III the realm begins its decline. The royal power becomes a plaything in the hands of the various political groups—the priesthood, foreign mercenaries, and Nubian provincial officials. The economic situation deteriorates, food prices rise, and the administration of justice declines more and more. The police power can no longer even protect the honored graves of past kings from plunder by conscienceless individuals, in collusion with the authorities in charge. Culturally and politically Egypt has played out its role as the leading great power in the Near East, and soon foreign rulers succeed each other on the Pharaohs' throne—Libyans, Ethiopians, Assyrians, and Persians.

Ramses III, the man who saved the land in its fateful hour, who granted it one final flowering, and who finally fell prey to the intrigues of his own family, proved to be the last great Pharaoh.

A meeting between East and West:
Herodotus' trip to Egypt

Herodotus, often called the father of historical writing, was a
Greek from the city of Halicarnassus in Asia Minor and lived
in the middle of the fifth century before Christ. He set himself
the task of depicting the great struggle of the Greeks against
the Persians—this fight which for us appears in a special light
because of such names as Marathon and Thermopylae, those
symbols of the West's fight for freedom against the barbarism
of the East. As is often the case, the historical truth behind the
symbols is not so simple and uncomplicated as the import of the
slogans has in time become, but this much can be said: that two
different worlds and ideals of life met in this battle, which had
decisive significance for Western culture.

Herodotus tells us that he wanted to write his book about
the Persian War "so that the memory of events of the past

would not be erased by time, so that the wonderful deeds of the Greeks *and the barbarians* might live on remembered."

This thought does not sound so remarkable to modern man, but it still reflects an entirely new spirit, an attitude which one might call typically Western.

The peoples of the Orient had also written the history of their lands, but often in a way that can drive a modern historian to despair. Basically everything is described in the same way, according to a predetermined religious scheme. Myth and history go hand in hand; and to the oriental, the myth is more important. Among other things, this entailed that his own ruler was a god, infallible and impossible to defeat. Enemies are always unfortunate wretches who get beaten and flee; this happens in every encounter, if one believes Egyptian sources, for example. The thought of also describing the heroic deeds of the barbarians—in other words, of the foreign peoples—as Herodotus proposed to do, was utterly strange to the ancients of the Orient. For them it was an article of religious faith that things could happen in only one way, and if reality did not accord with the ideal, one ought not to make things worse by preserving this memory for posterity. There are occasional exceptions, but these do not alter the fact that the whole basic approach of the orientals was to describe the passage of history according to definite preconceptions.

With the Greek historians a completely new type of historical writing begins, with a more honest attempt to discover what really occurred and, further, to characterize the persons who had taken part in the historical drama.

Here a chasm yawns between East and West.

It is difficult in a few words to explain the basis for this contrast, but we can see that around 500 B.C. something happened in Greece which was perhaps the most important event in the history of mankind. "The Greek Miracle," it has been termed. Briefly it can be said that for the first time in world history the individual is brought to the fore, instead of the collective, the universally applicable. Before, for example, there had been no interest in the personality of an artist, his name, whether he had a personal style or something new to offer. After the Greek break-through art history becomes a history of artists as well. Also at this time the concept of democracy appears, even though there was a great difference in practice between the democracy of that time and what we mean by the word.

Because of this spiritual revolution in Greece in the 400s before Christ, an entirely new type of man emerges. This was the Western individual, quite unlike the oriental man, who was tied to thousand-year-old traditions and accustomed to thinking and acting in collective terms.

It is rather fascinating to see what an encounter between East and West was like at this time, some twenty-three hundred years ago. There is no better illustration of this than Herodotus' account of his visit to Egypt around the year 450 B.C.

In order to give a reliable picture, Herodotus traveled to all the countries which had played any role in the great drama—the war between the Greeks and the Persians—and he therefore journeyed to Egypt to research the history of that land as well. Even this, of course, was an example of the new approach: to try to gather as much information as possible from the various primary sources, without preconceived notions. This would hardly have occurred to an oriental.

It was not really an appropriate time for such a trip. Egypt's period of greatness was long past. Seventy-five years before, the Persian king Cambyses had conquered Egypt, and terrible tales were still told of his wild advance through the land. He had torn down temples and told the priests that they could very well feed their sacrificial animals themselves instead of waiting for grants from the state. Why, it was said that he had even killed the sacred Bull of Apis, one of the land's most revered gods. Finally, for his own amusement, he had exe- cuted a few Persians in his retinue. How much of this was true, we do not know, but it is probable that Cambyses was a victim of political propaganda against his memory, intended in Persia

to strengthen his successor's claim to the throne and in Egypt
directed against the Persians in general.

There had been unrest in Egypt after the death of Cambyses,
and his successor, Darius, had initiated a more conciliatory
policy. But after his death there had been more disturbances,
and when Herodotus came to Egypt, a revolt had just been
crushed with heavy Egyptian losses.

While it is true that the Greeks had helped the Egyptians
against the Persians, in the final struggle they had infamously
abandoned their allies and instead made peace with the Persians. As a result, neither the Greeks nor the Persians were very
popular in Egypt at the time.

Now enters the Greek Herodotus, probably traveling with
Persian recommendations, trying to gather material for his
history through interviews, despite the unfavorable political
situation. He could not speak Egyptian, so he had to be content with what his Greek compatriots could tell him. He tells
us, to be sure, that he talked with Egyptian priests, but we
probably cannot rely too much on this statement. The higher
priests, at least, certainly thought it beneath their dignity to
speak to a barbarian like Herodotus. Moreover, he was a Greek
friendly to the Persians and, as such, politically untrustworthy
in their eyes. That Herodotus had no great comprehension of
Egyptian national ideals and aspirations to freedom, he shows
most clearly in one instance.

The last Egyptian king, he tells us, was taken prisoner by
the Persian king Cambyses. "Now if he had only had enough
sense not to intrigue, they would certainly have given Egypt
back to him, making him its governor, since the Persians
usually show respect for sons of kings . . . But instead he
thought up evil plots and therefore received his just due. He
was caught stirring up the Egyptians to rebellion. When Cambyses learned of this, he forced him to drink ox blood, and he
died immediately. This was his ultimate fate." So Herodotus
quickly disposes of the king who was certainly one of Egypt's
national heroes.

Herodotus could never achieve any real contact with the

leading Egyptians, and he was little more successful with the lower classes. He says himself that the Egyptians considered all who did not speak the same language barbarians, and elsewhere he relates that "no Egyptian, neither man nor woman, may kiss a Greek man, or use a Greek knife or spit or dish, and neither may he eat the meat of a clean ox which had been pierced by a Greek knife." When the Egyptians had sacrificed an animal, and invoked all conceivable curses on the head of the animal, so that the evil which might otherwise strike the sacrificers or the land itself should fall on the animal's head instead, they would then sell the head to a Greek tradesman. He was welcome to the head, and the curses were thrown in for free.

Now let us hear Herodotus' first impression of this curious land, where everyone turned him aside, and no one wished to explain anything to him, but which was still a land which charmed and captivated him.

"Now I shall speak at some length about Egypt, because it offers many wonderful things, and contains works which are more remarkable than those of any other land. Just as Egyptian air is unusual, and the nature of the land's river is unlike that of other rivers, so the inhabitants also have manners and customs which are the direct opposites of those of other men. The women go to the market place, while the men sit home and weave. Burdens are carried on their heads by the men, on their shoulders by the women. Women stand up when they urinate, but the men sit. They perform their necessary acts indoors, but they eat out in the street; they believe, in effect, that one should perform in secret that which is indecent, but necessary, but perform in the open that which is not indecent. . . . They knead dough with their feet, but clay [for pottery] with their hands. When Greeks write and calculate, they move the hand from left to right, but the Egyptians instead go from right to left. They are religious to excess . . . and always wear freshly washed linens. They circumcise themselves for the sake of cleanliness, but value cleanliness above propriety."

As odd as Herodotus thought the ordinary people, the priests and all that had to do with religion he found still more remarkable. "The priests shave their entire bodies every other .day, so that no lice or anything else unclean may be found on them when they serve the gods. . . . Twice a day and twice each night they bathe in cold water. Still other ceremonies, almost without number, have to be observed. But then they also have good days. They need not use up any of their own fortunes to meet any expenses, since their sacred bread is baked for them, ox meat and goose flesh is supplied daily to each one in large amounts, and so is wine from the grape. Fish, however, they may not taste."

The sacred animals of Egypt, which were worshiped as gods in the various cities, could not have amazed Herodotus more. About these and about all kinds of other religious customs, Herodotus has notable things to report. The outer manifestations, which he could see with his own eyes and understand through his reason, are probably reliably reported, but he was almost always a stranger to the motivating forces in Egyptian religion.

In many cases this was because Herodotus never had a chance to speak to the spiritual leaders. Even if he had talked with them, they would probably not have understood each other, due to their completely disparate attitudes.

One little story is quite representative. Herodotus wanted very much to find out about the sources of the Nile, but no one could give him any definite information. Then he turned to an Egyptian priest. "But it seemed to me," says Herodotus, "that he was only joking when he told me that he had definite knowledge on this subject. He said that there were two mountains . . . between the city of Syene and Elephantine [in other words, at the southern border of Egypt, near the first cataract]. From the midst of these mountains, gush the bottomless fountains of the Nile, and half of the water runs north to Egypt, and the other half runs south to Ethiopia."

Herodotus himself traveled up to Elephantine and saw immediately that the Nile south of the city also flowed north, and he learned a good deal about the further stretches of the river, up to the Sudan, where the Ethiopians lived. But what had the priest meant? Had he really not known the facts, or was he simply trying to foist a tall tale on a stranger? Neither was the case. The Egyptians knew the course of the Nile up to the Sudan very well. They had sailed there for more than a thousand years before the time of Herodotus. What the priest was presenting was the religious conception of the Nile—gushing forth from the life-giving ocean which existed everywhere under the earth's crust and from which the ordered world had once been created. From time immemorial they had retained this concept—that the Nile rose from this underworld ocean just by the first cataract on the Egyptian border—and this had become an article of religious faith which was not to be changed, even though one knew perfectly well that it did not accord with reality. The worlds of mythology and of reality were quite different, and the mythological was the more important, the dominant world for the Egyptians. They felt no great need to reconcile the two; they hardly recognized that the two were not compatible in rational terms.

Such an attitude seemed as strange to Herodotus as it seems to us. To him, it was a bad joke.

Herodotus, of course, had really traveled to Egypt to write the country's history, not to depict all the curiosities which were to be seen there in his time. Since it was so difficult for him to make contact with the Egyptians, he had to turn to his Greek compatriots. The Greeks had settled in Egypt around the 600s, some two hundred years before, in other words. Regarding this period, Herodotus could get definite answers to his questions. Here we can still use his account as a rather reliable source. But concerning earlier times, the situation was shaky, for there he had to rely on the stories of the Egyptians.

As a rule, he had to depend on folk tales or on what the Greek-educated interpreters could tell him. There were many fine stories, but they had little to do with history. For the most part these were stories explaining the significance of the old monuments—really the anecdotes of a tourist guide.

At Giza, outside of Cairo, are the three Great Pyramids. The

largest was built by King Cheops, and the smallest by Mycerinus in the 2600s before Christ. Herodotus learned that Cheops
was a terrible tyrant who only created misery among the people
and forced them to do nothing but build his pyramid. But
Mycerinus, who contented himself with the smallest pyramid,
was so good-natured that not even the gods could bear him,
and they plunged him into misfortune. Cheops was so wicked,
says Herodotus, that when he needed money he put his own
daughter in a brothel to earn some for him. She bore this, but
in order that she, too, might have a monument she asked each
one who came to her to give her a stone. With these stones she
built a small pyramid which can still be seen today in front of
Cheops' great pyramid.

In this way Herodotus constructed a sensible and human
(inhuman might be a better word) explanation of the pyramids, a purely rationalistic background. Herodotus never
grasped that the pyramids were monuments from a time when
people believed that the king was the highest god and that,
therefore, it was a religious act to build a pyramid. A Westerner,
after all, is something of a stranger to such a conception and to
this kind of practical consequence of a religious-political belief
in the divinity of the king. The contrast between East and
West on this point may seem less striking now, when you
think of the monuments modern dictators have raised to
themselves. But then the West has never wished to regard such
instances as typically Western, but rather as something foreign
and distasteful.

In the same way, Herodotus tells the story of a king named
Sesostris who was shut up in a house by his enemies. They set
fire to the house, and in order to make his way out the king
laid two of his children like a bridge across the fire. Thus he
managed to escape from the sea of fire across the bodies of
his own children.

An interpreter probably told Herodotus some such story to
explain a rather common type of Egyptian royal-group statu-
ary, showing the king advancing across twisted human bodies.

Actually this was a symbolic portrait of the king as supreme ruler; the bodies represent all the peoples of the world, who lie beneath his feet. This, in other words, was a universal image, colored by religion, of the king's—the god's—omnipotence, now and forever. But the Greek transforms the universal into the particular, into something which happened to *one* king on *one* certain occasion, and overlooks entirely the symbolic and religious meaning.

So one can see how East and West diverge on one point after another. But in some cases the stories of Herodotus have direct Egyptian parallels. Concerning one of ancient Egypt's last rulers, Amasis, Herodotus recounts a number of anecdotes. According to Herodotus, it was Amasis who instituted in Egypt the system of making everyone prepare his own declaration of his property to the authorities, a system later adopted by the Athenians. Herodotus found this a splendid idea, but then he was neither an Egyptian nor an Athenian. Before Amasis became king, Herodotus tells us, he sometimes stole in order to finance his dissolute life. "Now, when people claimed that he had stolen their property, and he denied it, he was hauled before the various oracles which they frequented. Often he was condemned by the oracle, but many times he was acquitted. Now, when he became king, he acted in the following manner. He ignored and gave nothing to the support of the shrines of all the gods who had acquitted him of thievery, for he regarded them as worthless, since their oracles lied. But he lavished great care on those who had declared him guilty of theft, since these were apparently true gods who had infallible oracles."

Even as king, he continued to enjoy high life. He devoted only his mornings, up to breakfast time, to pressing affairs; the rest of the day he drank and jested with his drinking companions, in frivolity and high spirits.

There is an Egyptian papyrus which tells of the same king's fondness for women and strong wine. On one occasion he made a real day of it and finally dozed off outdoors under a grapevine. "In the morning," we learn, "Pharaoh could not rise, because he was completely beclouded, and he could not hold audience for anyone. And the people of the court moaned and said, 'O, good Lord! What kind of mess has Pharaoh got into?'" But Pharaoh himself took the whole thing lightly and called in a storyteller. Then follows an off-color story—but here the papyrus is unfortunately torn.

This story might well have appeared in Herodotus' book about Egypt. On the universal human plane, when it was a question of humorous understanding of the frailties of man, East and West could meet and understand each other. It is there, even today, that contact is most easily achieved between the two worlds, East and West.

FROM EGYPTIAN LITERATURE

Books and scribes

The papyrus plant is a reed which now grows in tropical Africa and in isolated places around the Mediterranean. In ancient times it was found in great quantities throughout the whole Nile Valley and was used by the ancient Egyptians for varied purposes. The root could be eaten, and was not an unusual dish. The hard outer shell of the stalk, which might be the thickness of an arm and as much as ten feet tall, could be braided to make baskets and sandals or twined into rope. One could weave sails from it and make quite adequate boats by binding whole stalks together.

But what made this plant famous and caused the Greek word *papyros* to survive in our word "paper" was the Egyptian discovery of a way to make the papyrus stalks yield a writing material, a kind of paper.

The papyrus stalks were cut in lengths of fifteen or twenty inches and the hard outer shell was peeled off. The pith which remained was sliced into thin strips, as wide as possible. The strips were sorted with great care; for the finest papyrus, only the widest strips from the center of the pith were used. They spread out the strips, close together, in vertical rows on a moist board, and then placed still another layer of strips on top, with the strips running horizontally—at a right angle to the strips in the first layer. They then moistened the whole thing with water, pressed the layers against each other, and pounded them thoroughly to get both layers to fuse. No glue was needed, since there was enough sticky substance in the stalks to hold the layers together. But pounding and pressing alone were not enough to produce a fine surface, so it was smoothed with a piece of ivory or a mussel and was finally smeared with a kind of glue to give the surface a finish.

The ancient papyrus sheets are so well made that one cannot separate the various strips, so closely and securely are they joined, and almost never have both layers of the pressed strips come apart. Even today the surface is often so finely polished that a modern, pointed steel pen glides on it.

There were a number of different grades of papyrus sheets, depending on how carefully the papyrus strips had been selected. By Graeco-Roman times, in fact, we are dealing with something which reminds us of our own graded standards of paper.

The single sheets obtained in this manner—about fifteen inches long and eight inches wide—were not put together to make a book, but were glued to make up a roll of several sheets. As a rule, there were about twenty sheets to a roll; this was the standard size which came from the factory. For we can actually speak of factories. Papyrus was produced more or less industrially—not by everyone pasting together a sheet for himself when he needed something to write on. In the time of the Greeks, at least, its manufacture was probably a royal monopoly which played a major role in the country's finances and must also have brought in handsome sums as an export.

A roll from the factory was therefore about twenty-five feet long, but there was nothing to prevent pasting together several rolls, if necessary, for a particularly long text. There is an ancient Egyptian papyrus roll in the British Museum in London which is more than one hundred and thirty feet long.

Papyrus was never an inexpensive writing material. In Greek times we hear of the inflated prices of Egyptian papyrus, and even in ancient Egyptian times the situation was probably the same. True, no price lists have survived from that era, but we can tell nevertheless. Very often it is apparent that a papyrus has been used several times. Underneath the text we can see traces of an older text which has been washed off. (Such a text we call a *palimpsest*.) It was not only for temporary notices and the like that one took a used papyrus roll, washed off a text no longer needed, and used the roll again. Such an erased papyrus was not simply scratch paper; it was good enough to be used for letters and petitions directed even to highly placed dignitaries.

While there is no record of any rationing decrees, no one can complain of any lack of frugality in use of the writing material. Sometimes it may even have been carried a little too far for the writer's own good. We know of one instance, in ancient Egyptian times, of a man simply appropriating the accounts from his government office in order to make a new roll from the pieces. He wanted to write down some fine old texts, of which he longed to have his own copies.

Anyone who lacked such means of acquiring papyrus had to be content with what we now elegantly term "ostraca"—ceramic fragments or flat stone chips. On such ostraca schoolboys practiced writing, and the poor recorded their business dealings, purchase contracts, notes of indebtedness, and the like. When you paid taxes, you received an ostracon as a receipt.

To return to the papyrus roll, I should mention something about how one wrote on these rolls in ancient times. You sat cross-legged on the ground, with the roll in the left hand, and spread out the first part of the roll across the knees, which had to serve as a worktable. In the right hand, was your pen— a thin reed which you chewed into the shape of a tiny brush. Later came reeds which were sliced diagonally, and pointed, which remind us more of our own steel pens and which made it possible to write with a finer line.

In earlier times the ink was kept in solid form in small hollows of a so-called writing palette, and it had to be mixed with water just like the paints we use for water colors. Later on, ink was also kept in liquid form in inkwells. We don't know exactly how it was produced; the black ink was probably some kind of soot or lampblack dissolved in a sizing solution. For headings red ink was used—hence our word "rubric," from the Latin *rubrum,* "the red."

Originally the Egyptians wrote in vertical rows, from the top down, first one row and then the next row to the left of that; ancient Egyptian writing usually read from right to left. Later they went over to writing in columns, with shorter, horizontal rows under one another. This was also a feasible mode of writing Greek or Latin, Arabic, Hebrew, Aramaic, Persian, and what have you; and all of these languages have appeared in Egyptian papyri.

When one had finished writing the text in question, the roll was cut off to save the blank portion for some other use. If the roll were not long enough, the text was often continued on the reverse side. If you wanted to be particularly thrifty you wrote what you believed to be about half of what was to be written, cut off this piece, and continued on the reverse side. Sometimes the estimate might be wrong and there would not be enough room on the back. In this case, you continued on the first side again, where there was almost always some room left at the top.

Naturally it was not so easy to find a particular passage in the text on such a large book roll, but to simplify this jumble a little, the columns were usually numbered, like pages in our books.

In ancient Egypt the written rolls were often kept in clay jars—the first forerunners of bookshelves—and each jar had a list of its contents. Later on, partitioned cabinets were increasingly used, corresponding more to our own way of keeping books.

We know very little of Egyptian libraries in ancient times, but, of course, each official department had its own archives, and in the office of the vizier, for example, were preserved all the records regarding purchases of land and real property. In the temples there were special rooms for the sacred books, and we have a few catalogues, or rather book lists, from such temple libraries.

In Greek times the library of Alexandria in Egypt was antiquitys' largest, divided into two buildings, one with no less than 400,000 book rolls, the other with 42,800 rolls, only fifty years after its founding.

The Egyptians were always a race of writers, but in the 1500s before Christ, a burial custom was instituted, which as far as we can tell must have entailed a colossal upswing in the production of books, or rather of book rolls. It then began to be a requisite of a decent burial that the deceased have with him in the grave a so-called "book of the dead." This was a papyrus roll with a number of varied texts which were meant to help the deceased in the underworld and protect him from all dangers which might threaten him there. It might be called a kind of handbook and travel guide for the realm of the dead.

Naturally this custom caused a rise in demand for books and called forth a journeyman kind of book production. The colleges of priests, who had charge of the burials, probably attended to production and sales and earned good profits from this publishing venture. To make production more efficient, they did not wait for orders, but instead wrote out a number of copies at

the same time. In several places in the text the name of the
deceased was to appear, and here were left blank spaces, so
that the name could be filled in once the book of the dead was
sold. They were not always so careful about this; sometimes
one or more blank spaces were overlooked, and it is thanks
to this that we know how the whole thing was managed.

After all, it was reasonably certain that no one would read
the book, since it was intended only for the use of the dead.
For this reason the text itself might also be done carelessly.
The main thing was that the book should be elegant in appearance and that the many illustrations should be handsomely
painted. The most beautiful books of the dead which have
come down to us are often those which have the poorest text.
They saved on the cost of the luxury format by doing a careless job of proofreading.

In ancient Egypt it was usually in the temples that the
scribes received their training. There is one school for scribes
in particular, from the 1200s before Christ, with which we are
quite familiar. It was located in the city of Thebes, and there
have been found the pupils' writing exercises from the first
halting steps of the easy symbols up to the apprentice examina-
tions. The exercises consisted of long passages from some well-
known text, a classic which even then had a thousand-year
tradition behind it. The pupils had to write from dictation, just
as in modern spelling exercises, and for the ancient Egyptians
it was spelling above all which caused problems. It took years
of practice to learn how to write the old conservative style
correctly. It would be roughly the same if we today were to
practice writing correctly spelled English of the Middle Ages.
The teacher's corrections have been written in on these school
exercises, and sometimes we see indications that teacher and
pupil alike were oppressed by the heat. The pupils make a
great number of errors, and the teacher does not feel up to
correcting all of them. Occasionally the teacher may even correct some things which were right to begin with.

It was a hard schooling which the future scribes had to un-

G. *Eriksson*

Imhotep as a boy scribe.

Harvesting. From the tomb of Sen-nuden, Thebes, about 1200 B.C.

dergo, and to comfort the pupils, the teacher might dictate a writing exercise like this one:

"You should have seen me when I was your age. Then I had to sit with my hands in manacles, and by this means, my limbs were tamed. Three months I bore them and sat locked up in the temple. My father and my mother were in the country and my brothers as well.

"But when I became free of them, then I surpassed everything I had done before and became the best in the class and outshone the others in the art of writing.

"Now do as I say, and you will prosper, and soon you will find that you have no rival."

At times the schoolboys must have wished that they had chosen a less demanding course, and dreamed of how wonderful another profession might have been. The teachers carried on vigorous propaganda for their profession, and with partiality let their beginners practice classic texts in which the privations and troubles of all the other professions were portrayed in the most garish colors. As an example, we might choose the profession which held perhaps the greatest attraction for youthful minds, particularly at a time when the Egyptian armies were advancing victoriously throughout the known world.

"What do you mean by saying, 'The soldier is considered to be better off than the scribe'?

"I shall tell you how he must go to Syria and march over the mountains. Bread and water he has to carry on his back like a donkey. This makes his neck as stiff as the donkey's, and his spine becomes bowed. His drink is stinking water, and when the march is finished, he has guard duty. When thus he meets the enemy, he is like a captive bird and has no strength left.

"If he comes home to Egypt, he is like a worm-eaten piece of wood. He is sick and must lie in bed. He is packed home on a donkey, his clothes get stolen, and his servants run away.

"O scribe, don't believe that the soldier is better off than the scribe!"

At times it might very well happen that a young man could

no longer stand the hard discipline and would cut himself loose, to the despair and indignation of the teacher.

"They tell me that you are giving up clerking and plunging yourself into amusements. You go from street to street, wherever there is the smell of beer. The beer drives people away from you and deprives you of your senses. You are like a broken rudder on a ship, which obeys the rudder in no direction. You are like a house of god without god, like a house without bread. You are found climbing on walls, and you smash things. People run from you, because you bring them to ruin.

"Oh, if you could only understand that wine is destruction. . . . You sit in the house, surrounded by loose women. . . . You sit together with a girl, having drenched yourself with beer. You have a flower wreath around your neck, and you are drumming on your belly."

But one who applied himself in school learned not only to write correctly the classic texts with their complicated spellings. Mathematics, bookkeeping, and geometry—indeed, all the subjects useful in administration had to be fitted in. Naturally, like the diplomatic service, this also entailed the skill of formulating fine letters and reports. Among these, we might pick as a representaitve tidbit a document which brings to mind the familiar song "Tout va très bien, Madame la Marquise."

"The scribe Pa-uhem brings happiness to his lord Anhorrech.

"With life, fortune, and health! This is written to inform My Lord.

"Something else with which to please My Lord: 'I have heard My Lord's command that I should give fodder to the horses in the royal stable of the name "Ramses, beloved of Amon" and in the stable "Ba-en-Re, beloved of Amon.'"

"Something else with which to please My Lord: 'Regarding the farm laborers on the estate of Pharaoh, which is under My Lord's management, three men have run away from Colonel Neferhotep, after he flogged them. See, the fields now lie desolate on the country estate of Pharaoh, which is under My Lords' management, and there is no one who tills them."

"This is written to inform My Lord."

The fully trained scribe had a privileged standing in the community. He escaped physical labor under the burning sun and did not have to pay taxes. Moreover, as a rule the scribes were those who attained the highest posts in the community.

Thanks to the Egyptian climate, great numbers of papyri have survived to our day, particularly those which came to rest in the dry desert sand. What is there for us to read on these ancient papyri? Well, the question is not easy to answer briefly; it might almost be easier to tell what is missing.

The great majority have Greek texts, and among other things—in addition to an overwhelming quantity of administrative and commercial records—there are fragments of both familar classics and works by Aristotle, Sappho, and Menander known only through papyri from Egypt. Other papyri have texts in Latin, Aramaic, Syrian, Persian, and Arabic, and not least important, of course, in ancient Egyptian, from both the earlier and the later stages of the language's development up to Coptic, which still lives on as a church language even today. That so many languages should be represented on the Egyptian papyri may seem surprising, but it was not until the 800s after Christ that people stopped writing primarily on papyrus and went over to paper, made from pulp, which the Arabs introduced. In the meantime, all the foreign peoples who through many centuries, before and after Christ, came to Egypt as conquerors or as peaceful immigrants left their traces in the rich papyrus literature.

Because of these papyri, we have an infinitely richer picture of the Egypt of the Pharaohs and much more as well, for they also shed light on the spiritual achievements of antiquity, Near Eastern and Graeco-Roman, upon which so much of our contemporary culture is based.

In the shade of the sycamores:
of perfumes and love

In a famous passage in *Antony and Cleopatra*, Shakespeare describes the refinements which Cleopatra employed to snare Antony in her skeins when she sailed to meet him for the first time:

> "The barge she sat in, like a burnish'd throne,
> Burn'd on the water: the poop was beaten gold;
> Purple the sails, and so perfumed that
> The winds were love-sick with them; the oars were silver,
> Which to the tune of flutes kept stroke, and made
> The water which they beat to follow faster,
> As amorous of their strokes. For her own person,
> It beggar'd all description . . ."

Egypt's Queen Cleopatra, of course, had not a drop of
Egyptian blood in her veins, but her seductive arts surely
made use of all the means her country had to offer. Among
them, traditionally, was a copious use of perfume and fragrant
balms, even though we may never have heard of any woman
perfuming the sails of her boat.

There is an ancient Egyptian story which perhaps best illus-
trates the role of perfume as a means of heightening a woman's
attractiveness and even as the very symbol of her beauty.

It is the story of the two brothers. The wife of the elder
brother, like Potiphar's wife, tried to seduce the younger
brother, whose name was Bata. Like Joseph, the virtuous Bata
got into trouble and had to flee for his life. He went to a distant
valley and lived there as a hermit. However, since it is not good
for men to be alone, the gods created a wonderful woman for
him, and they lived together happily.

But one day, when she was out walking by the seashore, the
ocean god got hold of a lock of her hair and bore it with him
to Egypt, to just the spot where Pharaoh's clothes were usually
washed. "Every day, they scolded the washers and said: 'There
is a scent of perfume in Pharaoh's clothes!' And the washers
did not know what to do. Their overseer went to the washing
place, deeply troubled because he was scolded every day."
Then he caught sight of the lock of hair, lying there in the
water, and retrieved it. It gave off the most wonderful fragrance, and he carried it to Pharaoh. Pharaoh sent for all his
wise men, and they explained to him that the lock belonged
to a divine woman, a gift of the gods, from another land.

Pharaoh was immediately interested and dispatched soldiers
to fetch this delightful woman. But her husband, Bata, killed
the soldiers, and Pharaoh had to resort to a stratagem. With
the next troop of soldiers, he sent along a woman "in whose
hands had been placed all kinds of beautiful female adornments," as the text puts it. These, Bata's wife could not resist,
and she went back with the troops to Egypt. "The whole land

rejoiced over her. His Majesty loved her deeply and named her as the favorite, the great consort."

This tale must have quickened the pulses of many Egyptian women, oblivious to the moral ending of the story, in which the faithless wife was punished at last. To think that the wonderful scent of a lock of hair could inflame the desire even of Pharaoh, who had never set eyes on the woman! Dreamily, retreating into the mysteries of beauty care, they would bring out their cases of toiletries, containing the seven sacred balsamic oils. "Festival perfume, oil of jubilee, Syrian balm, softening salve, anointment oil, prime cedar oil, prime Libyan oil" were the seven fragrances. No holy ceremony could be conducted without them; they were rubbed on images of the gods and statues for tombs and used each day by every man and woman of fashion.

It was just as necessary for the Egyptians to rub themselves with oil as it is for us when we sun-bathe. The climate and the use of natron or caustic soda as soap dried out their skin. Even the humblest laborer had to be supplied with oil by his employer, but the refinement of adding perfume was no doubt limited to the more prosperous. It was as much a good husband's duty to supply his wife with such oils as it was to clothe and feed her. "Love thy wife, fill her body [with food] and clothe her. Balsamic oils are prescribed for her limbs!" He read in a famous collection of wise precepts.

A lady's cosmetic case contained more than the seven oils, sometimes increased to eight. Since many of these cases have been preserved, we know their contents quite well. There were several other beauty aids.

There was henna juice, used not only to color the nails of the fingers and toes a beautiful reddish-yellow, but also to dye the soles of the feet and the palms of the hands, as is common in the Orient even today. There was lipstick, made from red ochre mixed with grease or talc and a little resin. Particularly great care was devoted to the eyes. The eyebrows and the corners of the eye were accentuated with green paint, made from pulverized malachite, while a black paint, made from finely ground lead ore in a sticky solution, was applied to the eyelashes and to the edges of the eyelids. By these means, the eyes were supposd to acquire that higher sheen which was otherwise imparted, an Egyptian love poem tells us, only by happiness in the embrace of one's beloved.

The modern type of perfume was not available, because the art of distilling alcohol was unknown. However, oils made fragrant by the addition of various aromatic substances accomplished the same purpose. All the resources of the time were tapped in efforts to find the best and most fragrant elements and to fill the toilet cases with the necessary cosmetics.

One of the main components, oil of lilies, could be obtained from plantings in Egypt, and many other raw materials were found within the country. But they were not content with these alone. We are told that *Kufi*, which was the most famous Egyptian perfume even in Roman times, contained as many as sixteen different ingredients.

From the Libyan desert came natron and labdanum, which was also chewed to sweeten the breath. Labdanum cropped out like sweat on the leaves of a bush which grew in the desert, and gatherers would lash the bushes with leather whips, to which the juice of the plant would adhere. In the deserts of the Sinai and Nubia, hordes of wretched stonecutters labored to produce the malachite and lead ore needed for eye paint, and daring sailors risked their lives on long and dangerous voyages through the Red Sea to Somaliland in order to bring back myrrh, the most sought-after perfume for gods and men. Egyptian ships also plowed the Mediterranean to collect, among other things, oil of cedar from the coast of Lebanon; no doubt the Aegean world as well was the source of various perfume ingredients. In Egypt one is always uncovering vessels of Mycenaean origin, so-called stirrup jars from Greece, whose shape indicates that they can hardly have been used for anything other than containers for costly oils. During a certain period in Egypt's history, in the 1600s before Christ, small, black, decorated clay jars appear in great numbers, and these, too, were no doubt perfume bottles.

As the original containers, both the Mycenaean jars and the black ones, probably Syrian, were meant to assure the buyer that their contents were genuine. That this was one of their functions is indicated by the production of imitations of this type of jar, and, presumably, also of its contents. The perfume dealer of the time might well have advertised: "Beware of imitations. Accept no substitute," if the slogan had been invented.

Naturally it was above all at the great feasts that these elegant perfumes and other beauty aids were employed, both to heighten the festive whirl and to tangle one's beloved in the skeins of love. Let us visit an Egyptian worthy on such an occasion. Since we have an open choice, why not choose the festival of festivals, the Egyptian New Year?

Even Herodotus, after all, thought that everything in Egypt was rather upside down, and the New Year was no exception. Oddly enough—from our standpoint—it was celebrated twice a year, once in July and once in November. The July New Year was the one most like our own. The New Year then began according to the calendar, and this was also the beginning of the Nile's overflowing, which meant life or death, plenty or famine, for the Egyptians.

The last days of the old year were passed in anxiety and agitation, more or less severe depending on the degree of conviction that every possible devilish power was abroad and about. Only with all the aids of religion and magic could these evil powers be overcome. It was considered most unlucky to undertake anything during these days. The temples were cleaned out on New Year's Eve, and all the images of the gods were removed from their chapels. On New Year's Morn, they were carried back to their places in a ceremonious procession by torchlight, which was the preamble to the joyous feast day.

Everyone breathed freely, now that the eerie time had passed once again. Offerings in great quantities were brought into the temples, and the fragrance of incense and myrrh rose to the divine image. The higher officials made a New Year's call on Pharaoh. Spread before the throne were the New Year's gifts, which corresponded to our Christmas presents. This was a general inventory of the unbelievable quantities of art objects and other costly things made by craftsmen throughout the year for this occasion. One can well imagine that the pressure must have been great toward the end, especially since no one could work during the final days of the old year.

Pharaoh, in his turn, let the sun of his favor shine on his courtiers. Having successfully passed inspection, the heads of families could rush home to private festivities, wearing golden necklaces and other signs of favor. The father of the household was received with congratulations on his own doorstep, and now it was his turn to be attended, like Pharaoh, with rich gifts and many good wishes. It was proper then for the wife to wish her husband a thousand years of life on earth; on lesser occasions one was content with the more modest ideal of a hundred years.

The more formal observances were not very different from those of our own days. One might present flowers or simply New Year's greetings. The flowers were preferably from the god's own garden, where the priests in charge must have been as rushed as our florists at Christmas and New Year's. The New Year's greetings were more elegant than our Christmas and New Year's cards. As a rule, they were small, beautiful faïence vases, filled with some fragrant salve or oil. On the outside of the vases was inscribed "Happy New Year!" or rather, "May [this or that god] launch a happy year!" which god one chose depended on the particular religious interests and ties of the giver or the receiver, but there was generally a set formula which spared the well-wisher any thought.

Then began the great festive banquet, one of the favorite

Cosmetics case with mirror,
shaving knives, and perfume
vials. From Lahun

Imported perfume jars from
Mycenae and Syria.

Bronze mirror with ebony handle, inscribed in gold inlay:
"The Great One of the Southern Tens, Renseneb."
From Thebes, about 1800 B.C.

Making New Year's gifts. Painting at Thebes.
Fourteenth century B.C. From Davis, *Tomb of Two Sculptors*.

Lady with two maids. Wall painting from the tomb of
Zeser-ka-ra-sombe at Thebes. About 1415 B.C.

themes of texts and tomb paintings, which were meant to permit the deceased to share this epitome of life's joys through eternity's eternity.

In the places of honor, in comfortable armchairs, sit the great man and his wife, dressed in full-length outfits of the thinnest, most transparent linen. About their necks they have garlands of flowers, and on their heads, cones of aromatic balms which melt and run down into their wigs, spotting their white linen clothes. Every conceivable delicacy is spread on a table before them, and a young girl, a daughter of the house, serves the ceremonial cup of wine. The hall, with its garishly painted wooden columns, is filled with guests, the guests of honor in armchairs, the others on stools or on rugs. It is good that there is air conditioning—large screens on the roof which capture the cool north wind and permit fresh air to stream into the room. The guests are wearing the same beautiful festive costumes as the hosts, and the scent of the aromatic cones lies heavy over the room. The wine flows, and one or two of the women even eat and drink a bit more than really is good for them.

"Give me eighteen cups of wine. I want to drink to intoxication. My insides are as dry as straw," cries one of the guests. And on an alabaster amphora, we read:

> Wine comes with gold,
> and fills your house.
> Intoxicate yourself day and night,
> free from worries,
> while singers rejoice and dance.

There is something for all the senses. There are delights for the palate, and the ears are caressed by music. The eyes can feast on the acrobatic dancing of naked girls, and the nose is filled with a subtle symphony of scents from the fresh flowers and from the perfumes, with their heavier fragrances.

Now and then the chatter at the feast is interrupted by the

songs of the blind lute players, who sing of life's joys and festivities:

> Drink to intoxication,
> celebrate a wonderful day.
> Your life is delightful,
> until you depart for the grave,
> where no one shall forget your name,
> where your family greets you with the word
> "Welcome!"
> and you embrace your own once again.

> What a glorious day is this evening
> and tomorrow we shall say once again,
> "Fresh is the hour of morning,
> lovelier still than yesterday's.
> Because of its beauty,
> let us celebrate still another feast!"
> Rejoice without worries,
> while singers exult and dance
> to make your day a festival!

Outside the villa is the garden. In its midst is an artificial lake, surrounded by a tropical luxuriance of flowers and fruit trees. In the shade of a sycamore, the fig tree of Hathor, the goddess of love, lovers hark to the imagery and enchantment of love songs. The sycamore itself is a living being, the protector of lovers and postilion of love, who might speak seductive verses like these:

> The little sycamore
> which she planted with her hand
> moves its mouth to speak.

> The murmur of its leaves is like the scent of honey.
> Beautiful it is with verdant boughs,

overflowing with ripe fruit
redder than jasper;
like turquoise are its leaves,
like faïence its color.

It sends a letter to a young girl,
the gardener's daughter,
an urgent summons to the beloved:
Come, let us celebrate a feast today,
tomorrow and the next day,

three days in my shade
with your lover at your side!
.   .   .   .   .

Taciturn am I,
never betraying what I see.

In the shade of the sycamore, by the banks of the lotus
pond, the young girl confesses her love:

I am your first love.
To you I am like the garden
where I have planted flowers and fragrant herbs.
.   .   .   .   .

A lovely place in which to wander,
    when your hand lies in mine
    and my heart is filled with joy,
    because we wander together.
To hear your voice is the sweetest of wines.
To see you is more to me than food and drink.

While the girl compares herself to her beloved's garden, the
young man may liken himself to a bird, ensnared by her
beauty:

My calm waters are in turmoil.
A flower bud is the mouth of my beloved,

her breasts are like balsamic herbs,
her arms like arching boughs,
her forehead a snare of cedar wood.
> A wild goose am I, ready to be snared.
> My eyes seize upon her hair
> like bait in the readied trap.

And in glowing colors he depicts his beloved's beauty:

She is unique, her like does not exist,
loveliest of all on earth.
See, she is like a shining morning star
at the dawn of a fortunate new year.
Bright, good, and with lustrous skin.
Beautiful her eyes in glances,
sweet her mouth in speech,
she never talks too much.
Her neck straight, her breast shining,
her hair like the blue sapphire,
her arms with gold competing,
her fingers like lotus buds,
lovely her passage, when she glides over the ground.

In the ear of his heart's mistress, the lover may whisper a love poem with her perfume as its theme:

Oh, if I were your Nubian slave girl,
who washes your feet,
then I could contemplate
the skin of your limbs.

Oh, if I were your washerman
if only for a month
then I should be happy, washing out the oil,
which is in your clothes.

Perhaps she then responds with another well known verse:

> My god, my beloved, I am coming to you!
> It is delightful to wander down to the river.
> How glad I am that you wish
> to see me bathe before you.
>
> I let you contemplate my beauty
> in a costume of the finest linen,
> which is drenched in balsam
> and moist with scented oils.

Egyptian love lyrics do not neglect the universal theme of the lover who grows ill with longing when his beloved has left him all alone:

> For seven days, as of yesterday, I have not seen my
> beloved,
> and grave sickness has come upon me.
>
> Should the foremost physicians come to me,
> their medicines could not calm my heart,
> nor can magicians find a way.
> My sickness they can not fathom.
>
> But the words, "Look, she is here," bring me back to life.
> Better than any medicine is my beloved,
> better for me than a whole book of prescriptions.
>
> Her voice makes me strong,
> her embrace drives away my ills.
> But seven days ago she left me . . .

In another love poem it is the girl who calls upon her lover to return soon, in stanzas rich in imagery:

> Oh, come quickly to your beloved
> like a king's messenger

whose master is determined
to hear your message immediately.

All the stables are placed at his disposal,
he has horses waiting at the way station,
and his chariot is hitched up, as soon as it halts.
He may not catch his breath on the way.
When he reaches his beloved's home,
his heart leaps with joy.

Oh, come quickly to your beloved
like a gazelle racing across the desert,
with trembling legs and weakening limbs
with fright in his body.

Hunters behind him, dogs around him.
Now the cloud of dust is seen no more,
he has found a refuge among the reeds
and made his way along the river.

May you come to my cave
as quick as four kisses on the hand.
You seek my love
as ordered by the golden goddess, the goddess of love,
you, my friend!

In solitude, the young girl in love neglects her duties while
dreaming of her heart's desire, and she returns empty-handed
when sent out to catch birds:

The wild goose raises its cries,
snared by the bait in the trap.
From your love, which has snared me,
I cannot free myself.

And so I must take home my nets.
What shall I say to my mother,
to whom each day I came home,

burdened with captured birds?
Today I have not set my traps,
your love has ensnared me.

In the love lyrics of Egypt, as in those of the entire world, it is the theme of separation which strikes the most sonorous chords.

Wise as Ptahhotep

"Dotage has set in, and old age has come. The body has grown feeble and age makes itself felt. The powers of one who is fatigued begin to dry up. The mouth is silent and cannot speak; the eyes are weak, and the ears are deaf. One grows forgetful and cannot even remember what happened yesterday. The bones suffer from age, and the nose is stopped up, so that one cannot even breathe. The misery is the same, whether one is standing or sitting. All that was good has gone bad, and one has lost one's taste for everything. That is what old age does to man; it makes everything go sour."

Thus spoke the wise old Egyptian, Ptahhotep, four thousand five hundred years ago, when he beseeched his king to permit him to retire from his high post as the land's vizier, or prime minister. It was not so strange that he felt feeble and sated with years. According to the ancient Egyptian story, he served his master faithfully until the venerable age of one hundred and ten years. It was the Egyptian conception that one had to reach this age in order to attain true knowledge of life—more precisely, that one attained this after one hundred years and had ten years in which to apply it.

Such a reasonable request to be pensioned off could hardly be denied, but first the aged Ptahhotep was commissioned to instruct his son and successor in all the wisdom he had acquired in so long a lifetime. This course of instruction is one of the oldest surviving "books of wisdom" from Egypt. Like subsequent collections of wise teachings, this later became a classic text for the Egyptians themselves. For thousands of years schoolboys were plagued with these texts, and just as someone today with a classical education may enjoy spouting fine quotations, once drummed into him by his teachers, it was a mark of good breeding and elegant manners in ancient Egypt to decorate one's speech with phrases from the writings of Ptahhotep and other wise men.

To have "the wisdom of Ptahhotep" must have had about the same ring to it as having "the wisdom of Solomon" has in our own day. And, in fact, the time which elapsed between Ptahhotep, in the 2500s before Christ, to the last echo of his maxims, in a book of wise sayings which dates from shortly after the birth of Christ, is just as long as the time which separates Solomon from our own days.

The society in which Ptahhotep lived—the Egypt of the pyramid epoch, in the 2500s—was a strongly bureaucratic dictatorship, if one may apply so modern an expression to a time when individualism had not yet become a problem, and to a society in which the supreme power had been wielded since time immemorial by a king who was also a god—the highest god, or his representative, whose divine power was raised above good and evil, as self-evident as a natural law. "What the god commands is what comes to be"; and "it is the god who bestows a higher place in society," says Ptahhotep. As one might expect, the ideal which Ptahhotep, a man who had attained the highest station in society, wants to impress upon his son is that of the perfect public official, who conducts himself to the satisfaction of all, and who therefore advances rapidly and without fail. This is the flexible man of the world, who never permits musings upon life's deeper meaning and the more or less insoluble riddles of existence to disturb a good night's sleep and effectiveness on the job.

Toward one's superiors, one should show all possible politeness and studied submissiveness: "Bow to your superior, he who is above you in the king's service, and your house with all its goods shall endure, and you shall be properly paid." "If you are seated at table with one who is greater than you, partake of what is served when he offers it to you. Do not look at his portion; look only at your own." "Keep your face turned downward, until he greets you, and do not speak until you are spoken to. Laugh when he laughs; this will make a pleasing impression upon him." "If things go badly for you, yet you are in the service of a man of note, who stands high in favor, do not let on that you know his station to have been more modest previously. Take no liberties because you know how things were before. Respect him for what has happened to him—for nothing comes by itself." In other words, if he has got ahead, he must surely have deserved it—a conclusion which bears witness, in our opinion, to an almost naive faith in the ideal justice of the contemporary society.

When, through these and similar virtues, one has attained a leading position, one must strive for excellence, so that one's transactions may be without fault. "Truth and righteousness are the only things which endure, and he who departs from them will be punished." One should not be arrogant about one's skill: "Do not be proud of your knowledge, and do not be too sure of yourself, because you are learned. Take advice from the unskilled as well as from the skilled, for art knows no bounds, and no artist ever attains the whole of his art. A wise word is more rare than the green gemstone, and can be found even among the slave girls at the handmill."

What wisdom of officialdom is contained in the following advice: "If you are a man in an important position, be tolerant when you listen to a petitioner. Do not turn him away until he has presented all he wants to say. One who is troubled is eager to unburden his heart. If you rudely interrupt one who comes with a request, it will be said of you: 'What good is he, when he acts that way?'"

Once one has attained a good position, one should also know how to enjoy life and allow oneself some recreation. If one is wise, one marries: "Love your wife. Make her glad as long as she lives; then she will be a good field for her lord."

With other men's women, however, one had to be careful. "If you want to preserve friendship in a family to which you are related as master or brother or friend, beware of approaching the women."

One's own family and household should be well cared for: "Provide for your household with whatever you have. No one knows how things may turn out for you. If you fall into disgrace, only your household will still bid you welcome." You can just picture the disgraced official, sneaking away in shame from the palace under everyone's contemptuous looks, but finding consolation and comfort at home.

What is lacking among these wise teachings is any understanding or feeling for life's more irrational moments. Everything is laid out by a clear and chilly intelligence without any deeper feelings. With a logic not subject to appeal, it all follows pragmatic laws. This approach is perhaps most crassly apparent in regard to children: "If you are well off, and you have a son, one who is pleasing to god, who acts righteously and follows in your footsteps, who listens to your instructions, who conducts himself well at home and tends your property as he should, then do all good things for him. He is then truly your son, one whom you have spawned in your own image.

Pharaoh's favorite rewarded with golden necklaces.
Relief from the fourteenth century B.C. Leyden Museum.

The vintage.
Wall painting from the tomb of the sculptor Apuy. Thebes.

The rich man's ox is slaughtered.

A. Mekhitarian

African soldiers with feathers, and man with drum.
From the tomb of Tjanny, Thebes.

Papyrus harvest; splitting papyrus.
From the tomb of Puyemre, Thebes, about 1450 B.C.

G. *Eriksson*

The wise baboon, sacred animal of the god Thoth.
Victoria Museum, Uppsala.

Turn not your heart from him. But if he strays and departs from your mode of thinking, does not act as he has been taught, conducts himself badly at home, and opposes all you say, then drive him away. He is not your son; he has not been born to you."

This sounds cruel and uncharitable, but it must be viewed in its own context. Let us look at the matter purely practically, as the unsentimental Ptahhotep surely did. If a son were a good-for-nothing, he became only a constant source of expense, with nothing on the credit side, and by his impossible behavior he might endanger the standing and the livelihood of the whole family, by placing them in disfavor with the king. If the son were driven from home, only one man suffered, the one who was unsuitable and unteachable. Otherwise, the whole family, with all the household retainers—in other words, a large number of people—might be plunged into ruin.

This hardheaded wisdom of officialdom had its natural setting in a society in which everything functioned according to cold but clear rules of justice, with no irrational elements to disrupt the over-all order. When this setting was destroyed by revolutions and civil wars in the 2200s before Christ, a different conception began to assert itself. Righteousness and justice here on earth no longer seemed self-evident; man was not only a logically functioning machine, a perfect official. In the long run, even conduct which, on the surface, is completely blameless and which leads to rapid advancement is not enough. In order to endure, the public official must be a good man, not only, as before, in the eyes of his colleagues and his superiors in this life, but also in the eyes of the judges of the underworld. It is this thought, that someday, after death, one will have to answer for one's deeds, which gives a new direction to ethics and morals. To Ptahhotep, success here on earth was the most important thing—to become so wise that one's maxims would live on men's lips. Now happiness in the life after this one becomes the most important thing.

One must fulfill one's religious obligations with offerings to the gods, but this alone is not sufficient: "The righteous man's virtue is preferred [by the gods] to the ox of the unright-eous man."

Righteousness here on earth is no longer only the reasoned infallibility of the cold official. Instead, power now also carries with it strong obligations to take an interest in the weaker members of society. The higher officials, during the troubled times which followed the pyramid epoch, make this very claim in their tomb inscriptions, that they protected the weak in all the vicissitudes of life and not only in conjunction with their official duties. And in the texts of wise teachings, this is in-creasingly emphasized. In the 2100s a king tells his son: "Do what is right, so long as you live on earth. Comfort the one who weeps, and never deal harshly with a widow."

This mode of thinking survived through millenniums, and during the time of Egypt's greatness, toward the end of the second millennium before Christ, the deceased took along with him a "book of the dead," which contained, among other things, what is usually termed the negative confession of sins—in other words, an enumeration of all the sins which the deceased had not committed. This was a standard text, general in character which could be applied to any man, whatever his station in society. The morality preached in these texts meets the highest standards, and the ideals of life reflected here bear the stamp of the eternal. "I have not made anyone ill. I have not made anyone weep. I have not killed, nor caused to be killed. I have not made anyone suffer. . . . I have not done violence to the poor. I have not taken milk from the mouth of a child. I have not slandered a servant before his superior." Even animals are included in the category of the defenseless, who must be pro-tected: "I have not mistreated an animal." "I have not deprived cattle of fodder." One who can live his life in accordance with these precepts certainly deserves to be termed a good man.

Dating from this era, we have another wise man's teachings to his son. While the earlier teachings of wisdom had been put into the mouth of a king or of one of the highest officials, we here encounter middle-class circumstances. Ani, as the author was named, was an ordinary temple scribe. Since the mother in the family had to care for her children all by herself, we can understand that they were not among the richer families in the land, who always had numerous servants.

Here we encounter some instructions similar to those of old Ptahhotep, and also the new morality which had since emerged. But because the context here is less prosperous and secure, other strains are also heard. The family bond is stronger, and in Ani's precepts for living the command to honor one's father and mother receives its most detailed formulation in Egyptian literature:

"Double the bread which you give to your mother. Bear her, as she bore you. She had great trouble with you. When you were born after your months, she suffered still more, and her breast was in your mouth three full years. She felt no disgust for your excrement. She placed you in school, when you were to learn writing, and each day she stood there with beer and bread from home. When you have grown up, taken yourself a wife, and created your own family, think of how your mother fed you and raised you in every way. May she never have cause to censure you and to raise her hands in prayer to the god, and may he never hear her complain."

If we disregard odd aspects such as nursing the child for three full years and permitting school children to have beer with their meals, this teaching might very well have been written today, and it finds an immediate response in our feelings.

When the parents are dead, the son should continue to serve them with offerings: "Offer up water to your father and your mother, who rest in the desert valley. Do not neglect this, lest your own son do the same."

He should show his wife respect and not inhibit her actions and words, and he should be wary of strange women: "Beware of a woman from another place, who is not known in her town. She is like great, deep waters, whose eddies are unfamiliar to you. A woman who is far away from her husband, says to herself each day, when there are no witnesses: '[See] how beautiful I am!' It is a fatal transgression to listen to such talk."

To succumb to the temptations of the bottle is just as bad: "Do not brag that you can drink a lot of beer. As you speak, the wrong words slip from your mouth. When you trip and break your legs, no one will extend a helping hand to you. Your drinking colleagues stand up and say: 'Toss the boozer out!' And when one calls to inquire about you, one finds you lying on the ground, and you are like unto a small child."

A simple man without political influence ought to stay in good both with his enemy, should he come to call, and with the police: "Remain good friends with the constable in your quarter, and do not let him become angry with you. Give him something to eat when you have guests."

The less secure circumstances of the lower rungs of society also produce a deeper understanding of life's necessities and capricious changes: "Do not eat, when another stands alongside, without offering him something to eat as well! What is there that lasts for eternity; man, after all, is nothing. One is rich, and one is poor. Is food something imperishable? May not this too [someday] run out? He who was rich last year is a tramp this year. Great oceans dry up, and shores become ocean depths. Is it not the same with people? What they plan is one thing, but what the ruler of life [decides] is another."

This basic thought, "man proposes, God disposes," becomes increasingly dominant in Egyptian precepts of wisdom, in which the religious tone and the sense of personal powerlessness and insufficiency grow ever stronger, in contrast to Ptahhotep's earth-bound self-sufficiency.

Though one is poor, one should not despair: "[The gods] know whether a man is hungry or is sated. If you do not despair, your god will provide for you."

All is in the hands of the god, even death, and for this one should prepare oneself in good time: "When the messenger [of death] comes to you, he will then find one who is ready to go to his resting place [and who can answer]: 'Behold, one who is ready is coming!' Do not say: 'I am too young for you to fetch me.' You do not know when you will die. Death comes and steals away the child from his mother's care, just as with one who is old."

This text of wise teachings concludes with a discussion of a pedagogical problem which seems to have been of great interest at the time—namely, whether virtue and wisdom can be taught and whether there is such a thing as a natural bent. According to the old traditional conception, from the time of Ptahhotep, the question was not worthy of discussion. But others maintained. "You should not reprimand one who is warped [by nature]. Do what you will, each man is [nevertheless] governed by his own natural tendencies." Or as another text puts it: "Each and every one is what he is disposed to be. Fate and fortune are inscribed on his character in the god's own handwriting." There is no use in trying to make onself better than one is. If one's tendencies are bad, neither instruction nor diligence and good habits will help.

The teaching of Ani ends with a discussion between the father and the son about this very question. The father, who has taken great pains to formulate the rules of wisdom for his son, naturally cannot accept the son's quiet objection that the whole thing may still have no value, if he should not be properly disposed to live in accordance with wisdom. If this were the case, the father should have troubled himself in vain. He replies, therefore, that since one can tame all beasts imaginable and can teach the Egyptian language to Negroes, Syrians, and all kinds of foreigners, one should be able to teach one's son to live in honor and fear of god. He threatens his son with a whipping if he clings to his reprehensible modern ideas, and the whole matter ends with the son giving in, though somewhat halfheartedly. He promises to do the best he can but says that he is still too young really to grasp all of his father's wisdom.

Of somewhat later date is a collection of wise teachings which attracted great attention when it first became known. This is the teaching attributed to a certain Amenemope, who was in charge of administering the land's grain and naturally held a very high official post. A closer analysis reveals that large portions of the text, in both content and wording, correspond to parts of the Book of Proverbs in the Bible, particularly the collection in the twenty-second and twenty-third chapters, sometimes known as "the wise man's words."

This Biblical collection begins with the words: "Bow down thine ear, and hear the words of the wise, and apply thine heart unto my knowledge. For it is a pleasant thing if thou keep them within thee . . ." The teachings of Amenemope begin the same way: "Give over your ears to hear what is said. Give over your heart to understand it. For it is good to keep it in your heart, but woe to him who rejects it."

This is an old theme in Egyptian teachings of wisdom, which even Ptahhotep in his time had dealt with fully, in a half-poetic form, and this alone would indicate that the Biblical text reflects the Egyptian maxims. Among "the wise man's words" in the Bible we later find a series of maxims with an ancient Egyptian tradition, formulated in the same way in the Bible and in the teachings of Amenemope. For example: ". . . with a furious man thou shalt not go . . ." echoes a technical term which can be traced far back through Egyptian teachings of wisdom, for one who has not attained the harmonious calm of the wise man. Further, there are echoes of Ptahhotep's precious directions regarding table manners in dining with important people, and of the prohibition against plundering the poor, which was always given emphasis in the Egypt of later times. Even the Egyptian discussion about the point or pointlessness of instructing one who is seemingly unteachable has an echo in the Book of Proverbs' words: "Speak not in the ears of a fool: for he will despise the wisdom of thy words."

The clearest proof of the Biblical text's descent from the Egyptian teachings is in one place which caused the translators of the Bible great difficulties until the Egyptian text provided an explanation. The original Hebrew text read: "Have I not written thirty to thee in counsels and knowledge?"

Amenemope's teachings are divided up into thirty chapters and therefore end: "See these thirty chapters; they bring joy and instruction." "The wise man's words" in the Book of Proverbs does not contain thirty sections, nor do the words in question appear, as they should, at the end of the collection. Either the Hebrew author thoughtlessly carried over the phrase, or the Biblical text which has survived was only partially preserved, in somewhat distorted form.

In other parts of the Book of Proverbs, we find Egyptian strains, more or less directly related to the teachings of Amenemope. Common to them both is the strong requirement of absolute righteousness and complete faith in divine providence. No less than twice, Amenemope stresses the same thing which the Book of Proverbs 15:16 expresses in the words: "Better is little with the fear of the Lord than great treasure and trouble therewith." Or, as Amenemope expresses it: "Better is poverty in the hands of the god, than riches in the barn. Better is bread with a glad heart, than riches with troubles."

Who would suppose that an ancient Egyptian, long before the birth of Christ, had written the following words which express in a unique way the basic attitude typical both of Amenemope and of later Egyptian wisdom:

"Do not go to your rest with fear of the morrow. . . . Man still does not know what the morrow will bring. The god is perfect; man is imperfect. What a man says is one thing; what the god does is another. Do not say: 'I am without sin.' Sin is in the hand of the god, with the seal of his finger [i.e., only the god can determine that which is sin]. In the god's hand, nothing is perfect.

"Do not laugh at the blind man, do not ridicule a dwarf, and do not injure the lame. Do not ridicule one who is in the hand of the god. Man is clay and straw; the god is the builder. He destroys and rebuilds each day. As he thinks best, he makes thousands to be humble servants and thousands to be overseers. How will he not rejoice, who reaches the grave, safe and sound in the hand of the god?"

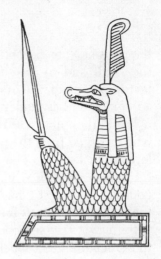

The fair-faced crocodile

In the broadest religious terms, worship of the warming sun, or of the whirling, ineffable vaults of the heavens and the heavenly bodies, is something which all men have in common, something which we find in all parts of the world. That one can find something worthy of worship in animals—a baboon, for example, which may have the look of an infinitely wise old man, or a cat, whose imperturbable independence may suggest possession of insight into fathomless riddles—even this a modern man can understand if necessary, perhaps not always with deep feeling, but at least in some moments of intuitive primitivism. But to choose so repulsive a beast as a crocodile to be loved and cherished as a divine protector, to be kept tame in the holy

241

temple pools, to be better fed and cared for than the poor of the land, and to be embalmed after death and buried with lavish pomp—to this, our capacity for empathy is finally inadequate, and as modern Westerners, we remain outsiders.

"Hail, thou image of the sun god, thou great bringer of light, who emerged from the primeval ocean. Welcome in peace, thou lord of peace . . . The king hath given thee this thy beautiful face . . . with which thou canst [in grace] look after the gods. . . . Mayest thou be merciful to the king, by whose work thou art today fair of face."

So read a few sentences from a recently published hymn to the crocodile god, Sobek, who was one of Egypt's most popular gods. To be honest, it sounds mostly like a hodgepodge. "The king hath given thee this thy beautiful face" and "by whose work thou art today fair of face" apparently refer to the king having made a cult statue of the crocodile god, to which the hymn is directed. Whatever one might call the crocodile, "fair of face" seems hardly appropriate to this singularly unappealing reptile. Nor does it seem particularly apt to call him "lord of peace," "a great bringer of light."

It seems a bit more to the point to invoke him as he is described in other passages in the hymn: "the powerful god, who seizes [his victim] more swiftly than the eye can see, who lives by preying, master of the river, lord of terror." We must begin with this aspect if we hope to explain why this repulsive beast ever became the object of divine worship.

Nowadays there are no crocodiles in the Egyptian portion of the Nile, but in ancient times the river swarmed with them, and they had many human lives on their consciences. It was natural then to resort to magic and religion in an effort to protect oneself against this dangerous, unaccountable power. In all religions, this very terror of the unaccountable and the overwhelming has always been a strong determining factor in the choice of objects of religious worship.

In the same way, we can also explain the worship of a series of other beasts, like the numerous lion gods. It was particularly the more dangerous and aggressive lioness who was chosen as a divinity, and these goddesses were generally worshiped in places where there were valley stretches in the desert, the natural habitats of the lioness. Here it was important to have good relations with the lion goddess before one entered her territory. The name of the goddess changes from one place to another. Sometimes she is called "the slaughteress," sometimes "the powerful" [Sachmet] or "the wild-glanced" [Miysis]. Both in these names and in texts which mention her, the emphasis is on precisely her wild, preying nature. One such lion goddess is called "the clawing," "the lioness with the keen eyes and the sharp claws, who catches sight of her prey at night and pounces upon it."

To have such a dangerous power on one's side was also to have a powerful ally against one's enemies. But there was always the risk that the ally might also turn her strength against her worshiper. There was always the feeling that it was necessary to conciliate the dangerous goddess and pacify her.

One myth recounts how the supreme god became angry with the evil race of men and gave the lion goddess, Hathor, the task of exterminating mankind. She began the slaughter with great pleasure, but the sun god repented and took pity on mankind. In order to halt the murderous goddess, he resorted to a trick. He had beer made which was red and looked like human blood, and he poured out seas of it in the path of the goddess. She was taken in and lapped up so much that she became totally drunk and could no longer recognize human beings.

The myth probably sprang up as a later explanation of a very ancient religious ritual, in which beer or blood-red wine was offered up, amid dancing and music, to appease the dangerous lion goddess. By this means, her character is changed, and she even becomes the goddess of love. Even the temple pictures of her change and become more anthropomorphic. Like many other animal gods, she is portrayed with a human body and an animal head. As a symbol of her peaceful nature, as a sign that the religious ceremony of conciliation has succeeded, the lion goddess now also carries a papyrus flower in her hand.

Due to such conciliatory rites, it becomes possible and appropriate to call "a lord of peace" the crocodile god, whose hideous appearance no longer strikes terror and may even seem beautiful to the faithful.

But this still does not explain why the Egyptians, perhaps more than any other people, should have selected animals to be symbols or manifestations of the divine power. This was a puzzle even in its own time, something which never ceased to amaze the Greeks and the Romans. They often made fun of these cults, particularly when all the members of a certain species were regarded as holy and were protected like the sacred cows of India. One Greek tells us that when a house burned in Egypt, no one bothered to put out the fire. Instead, they all positioned themselves around it to ensure that no sacred cat lept into the blaze. If, nevertheless, a cat happened to perish in the flames, they grieved as though for a dear relative. Should an Egyptian or a foreigner happen to kill a cat by accident, his life was forfeit and he was executed immediately.

No doubt some of these stories are somewhat exaggerated. However, if you were to see today the recently excavated place where the sacred Apis bulls were embalmed, with the great operating tables, beautifully carved from a large slab of semi-transparent alabaster; if you were then to wander around in the catacombs, where the sacred bulls lay buried in colossal stone coffins, of the hardest, highly polished granite, and were to see the incredible quantities of gold ornaments which once adorned the embalmed corpses of such a sacred bull—well, then you would understand that you really cannot understand, or in any case, that you cannot approach empathically the mentality which underlies the Egyptian animal worship.

Many scholars have tried to explain the Egyptians' characteristic predilection for gods in animal forms, but in my estimation no one has wholly succeeded. Some riddles always remain.

It has been argued that animals were chosen for two reasons: partly because man preferred something unlike himself, something which had points of similarity to him, but which was still a quite different being; and partly because animals fascinated him by somehow representing more clearly than mankind a changeless continuity, an eternal recurrence of individual beings without strong individual features. A city dweller, desk-bound scholar, might perhaps believe that animals recur as unvarying types generation after generation—cow as cow, lion as lion. But to a herder who knows his cattle, to a hunter who stalks his prey, each animal is distinctly individual and not simply a typical member of a species. For this reason, I do not find this explanation very satisfactory. Nor do I believe that the Egyptians were fascinated by animals because they were strange and dissimilar to man—at least not in historical times. The animal gods were then being humanized more and more, and many of the most important gods appeared in human form entirely. Gods who represented something abstract, or something not easily pictured, like air and water, were often conceived as manifesting themselves in human form. The form itself is then often inspired by the divine person here on earth, the country's king.

This brings us to an element which had enormous importance for Egyptian religion and strongly influenced its development, namely, the relationship between politics and religion.

During prehistoric times each locality seems to have had its special god, completely dominant in that area. According to some scholars, belief in god had its origin in a kind of "primeval monotheism," an original faith in a single divine power, which later split into a number of different, more specialized gods. The theory can hardly be proven—in any case, not with Egyptian material. To tell the truth, we know nothing about the precise standing of the earliest gods, whether each one in its own locality represented the entire divine power, or was simply more powerful than a series of lesser gods.

On the other hand, we have good reason to believe that every such locality or tribe was governed by a chief, regarded as more or less divine and working intimately with the local god. This produced two possibilities. Either the king took the form of the local god, or the local god took the form of the king. If the local god were an animal, it followed that either the king acted in the guise of the animal and was so portrayed, or the local god performed in the guise of the king and was depicted in the shape of a man, with the royal symbols—scepter, crown, and the like. In this way, we get a number of local gods in purely human form.

But what happens when this kind of city-king or tribal chief conquers other localities? The simplest solution was for him just to take over the place of the defeated chief or king and go to identify himself with the local god of the conquered territory. But there is still another way in which to solve the problem.

We can best see it in a concrete instance, when the land was united into one realm under a king who came from the city of Hieraconpolis, in Upper Egypt. The local god there was a falcon, Horus, who symbolized the entire heavens—his one eye, the sun; his other, the moon. The king of Hieraconpolis was pictured as a falcon and received the royal title Horus, after the local god. Among the localities he conquered, there were several which also worshiped a falcon god, and there the problem was solved simply by declaring that the other falcon gods were the same as the conqueror's god, Horus.

Sometimes it happened the same way even when the locality's god was not a falcon. He assumed the falcon shape of Horus, but in ritual references a few details might still linger on, which reveal to us that a god, who had the shape of a falcon in historical times, had originally been a completely different animal. One such case is a falcon god called "he of the sharp teeth." Since a falcon, of course, has no teeth, this must be a survival from a time when the god was a different beast. In this manner, a large number of the local gods disappear, or, to be more precise, from the source we have, we can no longer build any conception of them.

Still, it is amazing how stubbornly the local conceptions of gods held on, despite all the strivings for unity, during periods when a smaller circle of official gods—gods of the state church, one might say—were completely dominant, giving their names to a series of minor local gods. The most important local god retained both their names and their individuality. They took their places at the side of the chief god, Horus, in the great divine troop, the official gods of the united land. They form families and groups which reflect political developments, as ever-larger areas are combined into administrative entities. The families are often quite peculiar, as when the ram god Chnum becomes the mate of the frog goddess Heket, or when the human god Ptah and the lion goddess Sachmet become the parents of the lotus flower's god Nefertem. The result is a series of different theological systems of divine relationships, with related rituals and myths.

In the official religion, first one and then another of these originally local systems becomes dominant, primarily as a result of shifts in the political situation. When a new city becomes the capital of the land, its particular religious teaching assumes first place. This did not mean that the teachings which had been dominant earlier were cast aside. Tolerance toward opponents defeated politically, and thereby religiously, was characteristic of ancient Egypt. When a new teaching soared up to the status of most favored state religion, the gods of the formerly dominant system were still acknowledged to be great and powerful. But they were no longer the foremost or the eldest, which was the same thing to the Egyptians. Instead, they were descended from, or perhaps only other names for, the new system's gods.

Since the gods were immortal, the various generations of gods all existed simultaneously. Naturally in this huge family any god could lay claim to supremacy over the others if he could prove that he was the eldest god, the original one, who had created all the gods. We can see how the spokesmen for the various teachings dispute this very question, and how each system which attains the upper hand takes over the earlier conception and adds its own as an older and more significant element.

Had they been content to take over the earlier system unchanged and simply to tack on some supposedly earlier generations of gods, we could easily reconstruct developments in detail and figure out one age layer after another in Egyptian religion. But it was not that simple. The various theological systems changed under each other's influence. Originally distinct gods are combined into one; either the new god receives a double name, like Amon-Re, or the name of the old god disappears entirely. The myths and conceptions connected with each of the two gods are coupled as though they pertained to the *one* god, ignoring completely the question of whether they would or would not fit together. As a result, wholly incompatible versions of mystical events and contradictory explanations of natural phenomena appear side by side in Egyptian religious texts, in a manner which strikes us as totally confused and disjointed.

It is all this which makes a majority of Egyptian religious texts incomprehensible. Hordes of different gods appear in the most disparate roles, now as powers of good, now as powers of evil, now as friends and helpers of the supreme god, now as despised and persecuted enemies of the gods. It is only an exception when you find some order, as in the case of the hippopotamus. Here they have allowed the male to take on all the evil as his portion and to perform consistently as villain and devil, while the female is always a good and beneficent power. A more typical case is the god Seth, who is evil incarnate, as a rule, but who also appears as the valiant hero who kills the hideous serpent which threatens to gobble up the sun every evening when it sets on the western horizon. Worst of all, the same text may allude to both Seth's evil aspects and to his role as St. George. It is very common for disparate stories of the gods to to appear side by side with no attempt to relate them, and the whole matter often seems pure abracadabra.

Yet for thousand of years the Egyptians drew religious inspiration, refreshment, and comfort from such texts. They were not disturbed by the lack of continuity and what we term "logic." On the contrary, the more explanations of the same phenomenon, the better. The more god figures and myths which could be woven together into a unity worthy of worship, the more significant was the god, the more inspiring was the myth.

While it is more typical of Egyptian religiosity that the individual's personal relationship to the divine powers should seldom find expression, we can sometimes also find these religious sentiments expressed in immediately pleasing, intimate, and poetic tones, as in this prayer to the god Ptah, the lord of the city of Memphis:

> Ptah, my heart is filled with thee,
> My heart is filled with thy love and love for thee,
> Like a meadow with flowers.
> My house have I built near thy temple,
> Like a servant, who worships his master.

It is also unusual to find this attitude, which seems so natural to us in a prayer, this sense of one's own inadequacy and absolute dependence on the divine mercy. We encounter it in the lessons of wisdom of the later times, but more rarely in the purely religious literature. A prayer like this one to the sun god Harachte is rather an exception:

> Thou solitary, sole,
> Thou Harachte!
>
> Thou, the suppliant's benefactor
> Thou lord of the sun city!
>
> Do not requite me for my numerous sins.
> I am an ignorant man,
> A person without sense,

> In my everyday conduct, led by my mouth
> Like an ox after grass.

When we read the more representative religious texts, we are constantly reminded of how little of the Egyptian religion we thoroughly understand and how difficult it is to feel any real appreciation for this muddle of ambiguities and allusions to various myths, sagas, and rituals. Lack of source material is not the problem; on the contrary, thousands of religious texts have been preserved. In fact, this wealth of material makes it hard to see the forest for the trees, to recognize the common basis, the typically Egyptian in this jungle of religious conceptions.

We may often make it seem more difficult than it was. We remain outsiders, because the various names of the gods and the religious terms do not give us the right associations, and the religious feeling contained in the words is concealed from us.

Let us suppose that we had very obscure notions about Christianity and tried, without help from other sources, to understand an ordinary psalm, for example. Here we find Jesus, Christ, the Saviour, the Son of God, God, the Holy Ghost, and so forth, and if we knew nothing about the inner relationships, we should probably think that Christians clung to an endless number of gods. And what confusion would result if the cross were known to us only as an instrument of execution, and we were unfamiliar with the story of Christ's suffering and its religious content.

It is frequently the same with the Egyptian religion, and very often we have the feeling that the allusions to different myths and the mention of different names of gods are only plays on different chords of religious sensibilities. Reading or hearing the text, the believer might be enraptured by the omnipotence of the divinity, which could find such varied expression, but the essential thing would not be the aspect of change, but rather the common origin and impulse behind the transformations. Despite the numerous gods mentioned, one senses that the Egyptians were not such a long step away from belief in *one* divine power, that the ruling god in the land might acquire a status—in terms of feeling, at least, if not of theology—not unlike the conception of god held by a less educated Catholic, with a dominant god, his son, the Virgin Mary, and a number of saints especially suited for particular functions.

In Egyptian history, we can see a continual struggle for power among the spokesmen for the various divine systems. Which priesthood walked off with the prize often depended on purely political factors, and the driving force in the struggle was perhaps not always only a firm belief in the superiority of one system over another. In every time there have been men—not least of all, princes of the Church—who have had a wonderful gift for believing warmly in something which served their own interests. It was profitable in the highest degree for a priesthood to have its teaching adopted as state religion. With this came both poltical power and wealth. By the state, lands and slaves were made over to the god—to his priests, in other words. From the priesthood were chosen the land's most powerful officials.

That a particular god became the most important of the divine troop might often depend on purely external political factors, like the choice of his city as the capital. It was so that Amon, the god of the city of Thebes, came to be completely dominant during a long period when Thebes was the capital of Egypt. Such a change of state religion might come swiftly; it only required an order from the country's dictator, the divine king, which might come as swiftly as the change in our day from the Lenin cult to the Stalin cult.

Nevertheless, there are certainly also cases in which the inner religious force of a doctrine contributed to its success and in which we can also see something of individual religiosity, free from political tinge. An example of this is probably the sun worship of the city of Heliopolis. This city was never the capital, and however skillful its priests may have been as politicians, it is difficult to see what trumps they might have held other than the force of their religion.

The nine gods of Heliopolis very early became state gods and were able to maintain this status throughout the political shifts of thousands of years. At their head stood Re, the sun god, he who had risen from the primeval waters of chaos and had created the ordered world. His first child was the air, Schu, and moisture, Tefnut; and these two spawned the god of the heavens, Nut, and the god of earth, Geb. To these gods were later added Osiris and his circle of gods, which I shall talk a bit about shortly.

Worship of the sun became one of the main themes in Egyptian religion, a worship full of joy and gratitude for this beautiful and fortunate world, from which evil and unrest were kept away by the life-giving sun, which blessed all things. From this teaching, Egyptian religion derived its optimistic light, with the unhappy and the menacing eliminated once and for all, or doomed to defeat. This was the attitude, also, which produced Pharaoh Akhenaton's famous hymn to the sun.

The Heliopolitan sun doctrine, like Pharaoh Akhenaton's teaching about the one god, the sun disk, Aton, represents above all the bright life, which more or less ignores death, yes, even suppresses it. But man has always felt a religious need to solve the problem of death as well. This is not a question which can be shunted aside, and man's eternal hope of immorality existed in Egypt as well.

The sun priests taught that after death one might ascend to the sun and voyage eternally across the heavens in his boat. But this teaching never acquired the same impact as the belief in immortality connected with the god Osiris. It was Osiris and not the sun god Re, who became the god of the dead and to whom man fled from anxiety about death.

Osiris represents a god figure which has always had a great power of religious attraction. He is the god who dies and is resurrected, the god who shares man's inevitable destiny to die, but who proves that the road does not end there, that it

Bedpost: mythological animal head.
From the tomb of Tutanchamen.

The good hippopotamus-goddess. Glyptoteket, Copenhagen.

G. Eriksson

Manicure, pedicure, and circumcision.

leads on to the realm of immortality after a resurrection and a conquest of death. The sun god Re also promised eternal life, but the sun never dies, the sun is not subject to man's lot—with him, there can be no identification. The human element is lacking, and so are the oscillations in human life between happiness and unhappiness, light and darkness.

Osiris, the saga tells us, was a good and just ruler in the city of Busiris. But his brother, the evil Seth, murdered him. To make sure that Osiris should never rise up again, Seth dismembered his body and scattered the pieces all over the land. Osiris' wife, Isis, fled with the heir to the throne, Horus, to the inaccessible marshes of the Delta, to escape the murderer Seth, who had seized power in the land. Horus grew strong, finally succeeded in defeating the usurper, and became the land's rightful king. To his original station as a ruler here on earth, Osiris could not return, any more than any dead human being can resume his place in life. But Osiris' wife, Isis, had managed to collect the scattered pieces of his body and, by magic, to give him back the gift of life. He now becomes ruler of the realm of the dead, and in his kingdom, all the dead may live on for eternity, all whom the power of faith, righteous lives, and the magic aid of religion have enabled to approach him and to identify themselves with him. This possibility was not the privilege of a few chosen ones, nor was it wholly dependent on external means. With his own power and through the god's mercy, each and every one could win himself immortality.

This religious conception took hold on all minds and was able to establish itself, although Osiris' city, Busiris, never was or became an important political center, and although the political power of the priests of Osiris could never compare with that of the sun priests in Heliopolis or of the Amon priests in Thebes. To this all the divine teachings sought to relate themselves, just as Heliopolis admitted Osiris and his family into the city's circle of gods. The city of Abydos, which was regarded in later times as the burial place of Osiris, became a place of pilgrimage for the whole land, to which all the dead also traveled before burial and where memorial stones were raised to them. Abydos became for the Egyptians what Mecca is for Moslems and what Rome is for Catholics.

Egypt is not alone in the Near East in having the teaching about the god who dies, but who conquers death nevertheless. The teaching has its counterpart, for example, in Mesopotamia's cult of Tamuzd. This Near Eastern faith in a god who dies, but is resurrected, who can grant man the sought-after immortality, is no doubt an important background also to the Christian belief in immortality, and it is one of the many examples of how our culture builds upon an inheritance thousands of years old from the Orient's bewildering and fascinating antiquity.

Physicians and the healing art

In the *Odyssey* we are told that once when the fair Helen was giving a feast in Sparta, feelings among the guests grew somewhat tense. But the hostess knew how to cope with this and poured a wonderful Egyptian potion in the wine

> That drowning cares and angers did decline
> And thought of ill. Who drunke her cup, could shed
> All that day, not a teare; no, not if dead
> That day his father or his mother were;
> Not if his brother, child, or chiefest deare,
> He should see murthered then before his face.

This wonder-working remedy she had once obtained in Egypt, where—as the *Odyssey* tells us—

> . . . Every man is there
> A good Physition, out of nature's grace . . .

No wonder Egyptian medicine enjoyed a great reputation throughout the ancient world, if such marvelous things were ascribed to it. It is said that the Persian king Cyrus asked Pharaoh to send him the most skilled eye doctor in Egypt, and Darius is supposed to have got himself Egyptian physicians because they were regarded as the best in their field. The famous Roman physician Galenus tells us that the Greek doctors of his time used to consult the medical writings preserved in the temple of the god Imhotep in the Egyptian city of Memphis. In Rome, if one were stricken with an oriental disease, Egyptian doctors were usually sent for.

We have still more evidence of the world renown of Egyptian physicians. In a painting in the tomb of an Egyptian physician from the 1400s before Christ, we see a Syrian prince who has journeyed to Egypt to visit his doctor, for whom his slaves bring rich gifts.

But this renown might have its disadvantages for the doctors themselves, even though the practice of medicine seems to have been less risky in Egypt than in Babylon. There the physician's hand was severed if the patient died from an operation. It was a part of good manners among the princes in the ancient Orient to exchange gifts, and then it might happen that Pharaoh was more or less forced, out of politeness, to send a doctor as a gift of friendship to another prince.

Of the eye doctor mentioned previously, the Greek historian Herodotus tells us that he was more embittered against Pharaoh "because he had chosen precisely him, from among all the doctors in Egypt, and had snatched him away from wife and children and delivered him to the Persians." In revenge, the doctor incited the Persian king to attack and conquer Egypt—in the year 525 B.C. We do not know whether the story is true, but in an Egyptian inscription of the time we actually hear of an Egyptian doctor who aided the Persian conquerors in every way. As a reward the Persian king appointed him chief physician in the city of Sais—a city long renowned as a center of the healing arts. Later on, the Persians commissioned him to re-establish the medical school there, and he tells of this in his inscription:

"I provided [the school] with pupils. They were sons of important people, and no poor sons were found among them. I placed them under the supervision of all the wise men. His Majesty commanded me to give them all that they required, and I gave them everything, and instruments according to the texts. His Majesty did this because he understood the importance of this art, when it came to saving the lives of the sick and to making secure the names of the gods, their temples and incomes, so that the divine festivals may always be celebrated."

Here, for the first time, we are given a few details about a medical school, "The House of Life," as it was called. It surprises us a little that there one should also be involved with the gods and their festivals, but medicine and magic were not always carefully differentiated in ancient Egypt. As a rule, physicians were also priests of the goddess Sachmet, the wild lion goddess, who might permit the pestilential wind to sweep across the land, and they were often also "sorcerers" and "conjurors."

Even in the earliest times, however, there were physicians who were specialists in various fields. Archeologists have unearthed a number of tombs which belonged to doctors who lived during the time of the Old Kingdom, when the Great Pyramids were built. Here we find a number of specialists' titles. One man was "court eye doctor," one was "court stomach doctor," one was "court dentist," and one is called "He who understands the hidden"—in other words, a specialist on internal diseases. There were even "excretion specialists"! All these specialists, who had to watch over Pharaoh's gracious health, were grouped under the "Chief of the Court Physicians."

Doctors were accorded great respect. From the king they

received richly equipped tombs and beautiful statues to be placed in them. A fine tomb in which to dwell after death was just what the Egyptians valued most highly; life on earth was short, but life after death lasted for eternity.

The common people had to content themselves with quacks and conjurors. It was something quite extraordinary to be able to go to a real doctor. In ancient Egypt it was believed that the dead could walk again and call down afflictions upon the living, if they had not been properly tended. One poor fellow who believed that his late wife was persecuting him in this manner wrote her a reproachful letter which has survived to our time. He points out that when she was sick he had, after all, called in a "chief physician" who had "prepared medicines for her and done everything she could have wished."

Most Egyptologists now agree that ancient Egyptian medical arts were probably at their peak in the earlier period, during the time of the Old Kingdom. A number of Egyptian medical handbooks from various times have been preserved, and we can clearly see that the oldest ones are the best in every respect.

Perhaps the most interesting, as well as the oldest medical book which has survived, is the Edward Smith papyrus. This is a systematic surgical handbook—the world's first textbook on surgery and, in fact, the only one which has come down to us from the ancient Orient.

In contrast to many later works, the book is organized systematically. It begins with head injuries and goes on to cover injuries to the throat, the breast, and so on down, like a textbook on anatomy. Here we find more or less detailed treatments of various illnesses and not, as in later books, a collection of prescriptions only.

Remarkable, too, is the fact that there is recourse to magic only in one case out of forty-eight.

Each individual case of sickness was carefully examined before the doctor made his diagnosis. The methods of examination are often surprisingly modern, and they are founded on long experience and simple observation. If a patient had received a brain injury from a blow, the doctor not only examined the head wound itself and checked for any possible hole in the parietal bones—among other ways by feeling with his finger for the same pulse which a small child has before his fontanels have grown together; the doctor also had the patient attempt certain movements and noted, for example, any kind of paralysis of the arms or legs, or irregular movements of the facial muscles. But just because the Egyptians had observed that brain injuries might bring on paralysis, we cannot assume that they knew the brain to be a center which controls bodily movements. At least nothing was said about this, and as a rule they regarded the heart as the center of thought processes and similar functions. Their knowledge of anatomy was not very great, but of the meninges, for example, some observations were made.

It was also part of the examination to feel and count the pulse. In the Edward Smith papyrus, there is a careful explanation of why one should do so:

"There are vessels in the heart," we read, "to all the limbs. If a priest of Sachmet or a physician lays his hand, or more precisely, his fingers, on [the patient's] head, neck, or hands, he measures the heart, because the vessel from it can be found there [in the head and so forth] . . . and because it is the heart which is speaking from all the limbs. 'To measure' means to measure this in order to find out what the condition of the heart is."

To a modern person this may not sound very remarkable, but it is interesting that before this we had always thought that Greek doctors, in the 200s before Christ, were the first to use this method of examining the heart by counting the pulse. Now we know that the Egyptians, several thousands of years earlier, had understood the functioning of the heart and had taken their patients' pulses.

When the doctor had completed his examination, he formulated his prognosis, his prospects of curing the case. He based the prognosis entirely on his observations in the course of the examination, and this has been termed one of the very oldest examples of pure logical reasoning. Three different possibilities are mentioned: illnesses which the physician can treat and cure, those which he can treat and attempt to cure, and those which he cannot treat—hopeless cases, in other words. In this latter case, and in dealing with several other rather complex diseases, the doctor is advised to wait for a crisis—to let nature take its course but to keep the patient under observation, on the chance that he might improve enough to make treatment possible.

It is interesting to note that no less than fourteen cases out of forty-eight are regarded by the physician as completely hopeless. But they are still described in detail, possibly out of pure scientific interest. In its time, such solely theoretical interest was quite unique, something which does not recur until far later on in medical history. The fact that the doctor recognizes his own limitations is another thing uncommon in this early era of medicine.

The actual treatment of the various wounds, and above all, the surgical incisions, are not generally described in detail. Often linen tampons were used, and the wounds were closed up with plasters of some kind.

As treatment for open sores, the textbook recommends that fresh meat be placed on the sore for a day, to be replaced with finely shredded linen, drenched in liniment of fat and honey. To cure an inflamation in a wound, an infusion of sallow, among other things, is recommended as a kind of antiseptic. In modern times, salicin and salicylates, also antiseptics, were originally represented by sallow (salix).

In cases of broken bones, various splints were used and probably also something similar to modern plaster casts. That the Egyptians were skilled at mending breaks we can tell from a number of mummies. We have over a hundred examples of mummies with broken bones which had healed properly, without complications.

In the surgical handbook no surgical instruments are mentioned other than the drill, which was to be heated and used for burning away tumors on the breast. But we know still another way in which the drill was used. A jawbone was found, approximately four thousand year old, in which an ancient Egyptian doctor had drilled a hole to empty out suppuration under a tooth, without harming the roots. Certainly it must have hurt, but the tooth was saved and is still in its place. Another example of the dentists' skill is a jaw of about the same age, in which a loose tooth had been anchored to the nearest healthy tooth by a fine gold thread.

From linguistic evidence we can determine that this earliest of surgical textbooks dates from about 2700–2500 years before Christ, while the copy which we have is about a thousand years younger. With its sober, matter-of-fact approach, it gives a rather modern impression, particularly when compared to the later Egyptian handbooks, dealing with other afflictions.

These are great collections of prescriptions. One of them, the Ebers papyrus, includes no less than eight hundred seventy-seven prescriptions. This is also the oldest of the collections, the only one which still contains some more detailed descriptions of ills. Pure magic plays no major role in it. In only twelve instances are conjuring formulas employed as remedies, and these are usually rather hopeless cases, in which other medical means were of no help. Perhaps we should not be wrong in surmising that the doctor simply wanted to do something to keep the patient from losing all hope, and if the patient believed in the efficacy of the conjuring, it was probably not a bad prescription in many instances.

But magic came increasingly to replace pure medicine. At the same time, we can see the Egyptians searching for a medical remedy which would be effective against all illnesses. A kind of oil with a laxative effect—probably not castor oil— gradually assumed a very large role.

These later medical books were probably put together from older, specialized works and even from purely religious writings. The contents are therefore very mixed. They were in-

tended as a kind of vade mecum for the doctor and were meant
to include everything of interest to him. Then it was up to the
doctor to choose from the prescriptions and to find out which
one was suitable for each individual case.

We often have difficulty in really understanding many of
the old prescriptions, simply because we do not know what
all the words mean. Quite often we can see that a prescription
contains some active ingredient or another, but in other cases
the prescription seems to be nothing more than pure magic
and superstition.

Despite the fact that the quality is very uneven, we are
struck by the extent to which Egyptian medicine was still
based on actual experience, without any irrelevant and mis-
leading speculations about the causes of sickness. They apparently kept on experimenting with various remedies until
they found something which seemed to help, which was then
included in the collection of prescriptions. Modern doctors
who have studied those prescriptions which are in language
we can actually understand, have found that quite a few of
them really must been of some use against the ills for which
they were recommended.

Let's look at some of these prescriptions:

"A means of preventing shriek. Fruits (or seeds) of the
shepen plant, flyspecks, which are on the wall; blend; strain;
take four times daily; then it ends immediately." And this follows as an explanation: "Shriek, this is a child who screams."

This sounds quite incomprehensible, of course, and the
flyspecks can only serve to lend the whole thing a mystical
shimmer. But if we assume that the *shepen* plant is the poppy,
so that the child was taking opium, it probably had a good
effect—at least against screaming. We know that the Egyptians
were familiar with opium, and tincture of opium, after all, is
also called *tinctura thebaica*, after Egypt's ancient capital,
Thebes.

Another prescription is recommended "to relieve a surfeit

of food, when the patient's stomach feels heavy." It contains figs, among other things, and very probably had some effect.

Against tapeworm, the handbooks recommend an infusion of pomegranates, possibly of bark from the tree. The same remedy is still being used today by Egyptian farmers, and even modern doctors are familiar with a similar medicine.

In all the vicissitudes of life, one turned to the doctor, who was supposed to know how to cope with the most varied complaints. There were numerous prescriptions for female ailments—for various kinds of troubles of the womb and for simpler things like "Prescription for a woman who likes to lie in bed and will not get up." She received an emetic. The Egyptian doctor had remedies for sterility, of the man or the woman, and prescriptions "to prevent a woman from becoming pregnant for one year, two years, or three." If a married couple did not have children, the doctor was expected to determine which side was at fault. Something which naturally interested expectant parents greatly was whether they would have a boy or girl, and there were several different methods of determining this. One of them was the following:

"You should put wheat and barley in linen bags, mixed with dates and sand, and the woman should cast her water over it every day. . . . If the wheat grows, it will be a boy. If the barley grows, it will be a girl. If neither grows, she will not give birth."

The same method, described in similar words, is encountered again in Byzantine medical books and also later in European medical books from the sixteenth and seventeenth centuries. About its reliability, however, I prefer to say nothing.

We know that Cleopatra bathed in ass's milk to make herself beautiful, and beauty care had ancient traditions in Egypt. In the medical books we find many prescriptions to make the skin lovely and to prevent falling hair. One such remedy might be worth passing on:

"A means of getting the hair to grow—one prepared for

Queen Shesh, mother of His Majesty, the blessed Teti. Leg of dog, date seeds, hoof of donkey; cook thoroughly with oil in a bowl. Rub on."

As though this were not enough, the doctor could also help a lady against her rivals:

"A means of making hair fall out: burned ^{c}an ^{c}art worm, cooked with ordinary oil and with balanitis oil. Apply to the head of the hated woman." Undeniably, a rather refined prescription, if it carried out its promise.

The doctor was also supposed to have remedies against rats in the house, against lice and fleas, against fly stings and bug bites. And if some poor fellow came to him, believing himself persecuted by the evil spirits of the dead, the doctor had various kinds of incense and ointments which would help.

Modern assessments of the medical skills of ancient Egypt have varied a great deal. Some scholars have ascribed to the Egyptians such profound insights that even modern medicine might learn a good deal from them. Others are of the opinion that the Egyptian doctors were profoundly ignorant of all that the art of medicine consists of. The truth is probably somewhere in the middle.

Egyptian doctors were children of their time and did not trouble themselves too much to differentiate magic and medicine. Moreover, their knowledge of anatomy does not seem to have been very deep. In Egypt, we are meeting the art of medicine in its very earliest childhood, and surely we must admit that it was a very precocious child. For a long time afterward, the art of medicine was not to advance much further, and superstition would often exercise a wider influence than Egyptian medicine, which, on the whole, and particularly in the earliest times, was at least built on actual experience, without too many irrelevant speculations.

Without exaggerating, one can say that folk medicine both in the Orient and Europe was largely built on the legacy from Egypt. In Egypt we encounter for the first time many of the drugs which were universally used in the same way in later times—for example, tartar salt, castor oil and other oils with laxative effects, caraway and dill. From Egypt they were taken over by Greek and Roman doctors, and eventually they reappeared in the European medical books of the Middle Ages and subsequent times. There are prescriptions which have stayed the same, almost word for word, throughout the ages. And the best method of setting a broken jaw can be found, described in the same way, in both the ancient Egyptian surgical handbook and in the writings of the famous Greek physician Hippocrates.

In modern Egyptian folk medicine we have a direct survival from ancient Egyptian medicine. As an example, we might note that an ancient Egyptian prescription, (from the 1500s before Christ)—to use sycamore sap on a bleeding wart or pimple —is still in use among the Egyptian peasants. The same is true of bat blood as a means of hindering the growth of hair.

It is really not so strange that an effective remedy hit upon by the ancient Egyptians should survive into modern times. The tradition was never completely broken, and generation learned from generation down through millenniums. But the fact that utterly meaningless and ineffective prescriptions have been copied out slavishly for thousands of years is perhaps the best sign of the high standing of ancient Egyptian medicine and of the reputation it must once have enjoyed. What better tribute can an authority receive than to have even his stupidities survive and exert influence for thousands of years?

FROM CHRISTIAN TIMES

The flight into Egypt

From the Gospel of St. Matthew we learn that when the three
wise men had hailed the infant Jesus and returned to their
own country, ". . . behold, the angel of the Lord appeareth
to Joseph in a dream, saying, Arise, and take the young child
and his mother, and flee into Egypt, and be thou there until
I bring thee word; for Herod will seek the young child to
destroy him. When he arose, he took the young child and his
mother by night, and departed into Egypt: And was there
until the death of Herod . . ." In this manner, the infant Jesus
escaped the slaughter of the children in Bethlehem. When
Herod was dead, Joseph received God's command to return
to Israel, and they settled then in Nazareth.

271

Herod had come to power with the help of the Roman, Marcus Antonius, much to the indignation of the Egyptian queen, Cleopatra; and in Palestine he ruled as a more or less independent king. In Egypt, however, he had no authority and therefore could not have the Holy Family handed over as political refugees. Egypt in this era was a Roman province, regarded as the Emperor's private property, on which no Roman senator might set foot.

Anyone who came to Egypt in Jesus' time did not have to be there long in order to notice that the Jews played an important role in the country. Here lived every conceivable people and race. Aside from the Egyptians themselves, there were great numbers of Greeks, many Romans, Nubians, Persians, and even Indians. But the Jews were one of the largest foreign-population groups. No less than a million Jews are supposed to have lived there at the time of Jesus, and since the traffic on the Nile was watched over by Jewish customs men and police, Jews were the first people encountered on a visit to Egypt.

Throughout the country their political rights were at least as great as those of the Egyptians themselves, and in some areas they constituted a class with special privileges. If you had traveled from the border some distance into the country and had come to the city of Leontopolis, now called "the hill of the Jews," you would have found there a great temple consecrated to Jahve. It was built as a smaller copy of King Solomon's temple in Jerusalem, and rich lands belonged to the temple. To the orthodox Jews, it was probably an abomination, since they felt that Jahve should have only one temple, the one in Jerusalem.

The temple in Leontopolis had come into existence in the following way. The high priests in Jerusalem had become dependent on the Seleucid kings in Syria, and in the 150s before Christ, the one who was actually supposed to become high priest fled to Egypt. There, he was received with open arms by the king, not least for the purpose of enraging his political opponent in Syria. The high priest was given both land and

money to build a temple to compete with the temple in Jerusalem, which had fallen into some disrepute because of political
intrigues.

What had happened was nothing new, either in Egypt's
history or in Judaism's. Even in much earlier times there had
been Jews in Egypt. Above all, they were farmers and soldiers,
and already when the Persians ruled Egypt, in the 400s before
Christ, Jewish soldiers had been used as border guards in the
south. The Jewish military colony in the border city of Elephantine had also constructed a temple to Jahve, and the Jews had
such great political power in this part of the land that the
Egyptians and the Persian governor finally reacted against it
and had the Jahve temple torn down in the year 410. But so
strong and influential were the Jews, even in that time, that
all those who played leading roles in the destruction of the
temple had without exception lost their lives within two years
after the event.

When, later, Egypt was conquered by Alexander the Great
and acquired Greek kings, the so-called Ptolemies, the Jews
got a still more favored status, and more and more immigrated.
Many of them settled in the new capital, Alexandria, where
they were given the same privileged status as the Greek
Alexandrians. They were cared for in every way by the
Ptolemaic kings, and they were even given certain privileges
out in the provinces. In addition to the temple in Leontopolis,
there were plenty of synagogues in the land, in which refugees
could even find escape from the hands of the law, since the
synagogues had the right of asylum.

Now and then there might come persecutions of the Jews,
who were still for the most part soldiers and who therefore
readily got involved in internal political intrigues. One queen,
who fought for her son's right to the throne, had two Jewish
generals commanding her entire army. When she lost the
fight, the victor permitted his revenge to extend to all the Jews.
According to one Jewish tale, he set his war elephants on the
Jews; however, the elephants managed to trample the king's

own men instead. After the king's mistress interceded on their behalf, the Jews were given back their favored status, and each year they celebrated a feast of thanksgiving for the miraculous deliverance.

When the Romans conquered Egypt, the Jews realized at a very early stage whose hour had struck and ranged themselves wholeheartedly on the side of the Romans, calling forth great bitterness among the Greek Alexandrians. It is indicative of the Jews' position of power in the land that it was in large part due to their benevolent attitude that the relief troops were able to reach Caesar, when he and Cleopatra had become sealed off in Alexandria by his political opponents. Caesar and his successors showed their gratitude, and in Jesus' time the status of the Jews in Egypt was better than ever.

In the capital city of Alexandria, two districts of the city were termed "Jewish." One, called Delta, lay on the outskirts of the city, beyond the harbor. Heathen slanderers claimed that it was a slum quarter, in which the Jews lived among the trash heaps outside the harbor, but to this a Jew might answer that it was an elegant district in which to live. After all, they lived right next to the royal palace. It was no ghetto, since the Jews lived there of their own free will, and many of them lived in other parts of the city. They constituted a kind of state within the state, with their own administration, their own officials, and even the privilege of receiving floggings only at the hands of their own administrators of punishment. A Jew from a somewhat later time recounts with great indignation that the Jews in the city had once been just as badly treated as the Egyptian scum, had even been flogged with the same sort of whip as they, which had never happened before, and furthermore, the punishment had not been executed by Jews. The Jews did not have any great respect for the Egyptians, whom they looked down upon with sublime disdain, both because of their inferior political and social status and because of their religion, which to Jewish eyes seemed more than permissibly ridiculous and baroque.

Their own faith the Jews always held high, and extremely few ever went over to other teachings. Pecuniarily, too, they sacrificed a great deal for their religion, and many inscriptions give testimony of pious bequests to the synagogues. The synagogue in Alexandria was one of the most splendid in the entire Roman Empire, and, according to the description in the Talmud, it was so large that the rabbi could not be heard by the entire congregation. Another man, standing halfway down the length of the synagogue, had to give signals with a flag when it was time for the congregation to say "Amen."

The connection with Jerusalem was still maintained, despite the Jahve temple in Leontopolis, and each year the temple tax was collected among the Jews and sent to Jerusalem. And when a Jewish rabbi in Egypt wanted to marry, an inquiry was sent to the archives in Jerusalem to find out whether the proposed wife was of pure Jewish blood.

Despite all this, a Jew from Palestine must have felt rather like a foreigner among his friends in Egypt. Hebrew and Aramaic might still be spoken by one or another, but the great majority had gone over to speaking Greek. Furthermore, the holy scriptures had been translated into Greek, and since the Greek translation was regarded as having been divinely inspired, there was no longer any need to trouble oneself so much over the original Hebrew text. Outside of a few orthodox circles, Greek had also become the language of religious services. Egyptian converts read the holy texts in Egyptian, but this was not really considered quite orthodox.

When one considers these political and social conditions, it seems quite obvious that Joseph should have fled with Mary and Jesus to Egypt in particular. This only meant moving to another place in the great realm of Judaism, foreign perhaps in many ways, but a secure refuge among well-placed and politically powerful friends.

However, there is one small detail in the evangel which indicates that Matthew probably did not see it this way at all. The favorable political and social conditions in Egypt are not referred to by a single word. Rather, the contrary is suggested. It says that Jesus and his family were to flee to Egypt so that the words of Hosea, "Out of Egypt have I called my son," might be fulfilled. This is an allusion to Israel's captivity in Egypt, and from this standpoint Egypt's land was not a place of refuge from something evil, but rather a place of degradation where the holy calling, the role of salvation of the world which God had determined, might come to nothing. In this sense, the flight into Egypt takes on the character of a test and a temporary abasement. This conception, of course, accords badly with the actual status of the Jews in Egypt in Jesus' time, when far from languishing in captivity, they enjoyed a privileged position both religiously and politically.

Why then this allusion, which seems rather curious to us, to the people's degradation in Egyptian captivity?

To understand this, we must look at the context in which the story appears in the evangel. Just after it, comes the account of the baptism by John and the beginning of Jesus' work as a teacher, a passage which culminates in the mighty words of the Sermon on the Mount. From the oriental point of view, the baptism can be regarded as the installation in office, and the Sermon on the Mount as its proclamation. If we translate this to the royal sphere, it becomes the various phases of the coronation with a rite of purification and speech from the throne. To a modern person this analogy may seem far-fetched, but in its own time it seemed natural and close-at-hand. The age-old conceptions associated with the king's role as a god or a son of god here on earth had not been forgotten by the time of Jesus, and the forms of religious expression were still influenced to a great extent by this tradition.

What does the flight into Egypt become from this standpoint? It is a common saga motif that the hero must undergo severe trials before his final triumph, but in the Orient this motif had a very special significance because of its connection with the divine kingship here on earth.

If we remind ourselves of that Egyptian myth which is most

typical perhaps and most fundamental for the ideology of kingship, what I mean may be more clear. This is the myth which concerns the gods Osiris, Seth, and Horus. Osiris ruled over Egypt during the time of the gods. He was a good ruler, a good shepherd for his people, a god who guaranteed rich harvests and everything men could desire. He was murdered by his brother Seth, but his wife, Isis, managed to bring him to life again. By the resurrected Osiris she had a son, Horus, the rightful heir to the throne here on earth. Osiris becomes the god of the realm of the dead, and Horus fights with his uncle, the royal assassin, Seth, over the Egyptian crown. Seth—like Herod in the evangel—learns that a king has been born and seeks the child's life. Isis flees with the babe to the impenetrable marshes of the Delta, and there Horus grows strong, until the time is ripe for him to take up the fight. After many years of concealment and after hard battles with Seth, he conquers at last, and he is proclaimed and crowned king in the land.

During the entire long history of Egypt this was a living myth with firm roots in ritual. Every new king who ascended the throne was regarded as a Horus who had triumphed over the evil powers, and each king who died was an Osiris. Even the Greek kings and the Roman emperors were regarded by the Egyptians as Horuses and were worshiped as such. When Jesus fled from Herod into Egypt, in other words, a Horus ruled in the land, a king who was identical to the god who saved his life by fleeing from an unrighteous ruler.

Is the flight into Egypt then an Egyptian aspect of the evangel, and was Matthew's account inspired by Egyptian sources? Of course not. The same, or similar, conceptions were found everywhere in the Orient, surviving either in religious rites or simply as literary forms.

This age-old royal tradition, dimly seen in Matthew's account, which views the flight into Egypt as a test and Egypt as a place of degradation, was not picked up to any great extent in the later legends concerning the childhood of Jesus. To be sure, there are some legends like the one of how Jesus subdued four dragons during the desert crossing to Egypt, how they came racing forth from a cave as the Holy Family neared and ended up adoring Jesus and disappearing. This story in itself would accord well with the older beliefs about the king conquering the powers of chaos before ascending the throne, but this was hardly what the pious creator of the legend had in mind. Moreover, this legend is of too late a date.

When Egypt became Christian, the fact that Jesus had once visited their land had a special value for the Egyptian Christians. Around this simple fact a rich structure of legend springs up, in Egypt above all. A number of the legends certainly go back to an ancient word-of-mouth tradition, while others are the fantasies of later times.

Even in the desert Jesus began to work miracles, and this was the scene of the legend of how Jesus induced a date palm to bend its crown to the ground so that Mary might pick its dates. The tree's reward is to have an angel of the Lord, at Jesus' command, carry off one of its branches to paradise. "This blessing I grant thee," says the infant Jesus to the palm, "that it shall be said of all those who are victorious in a good fight: 'You have won the palm of victory.' "

When Jesus and Mary were forced to pass the night in a pagan temple, in which there were three hundred sixty-five images of the gods, one for each day of the year, all the images fell down and broke into pieces. Joseph and Mary feared that the pagans would be outraged because the infant Jesus had broken their images, but when the mayor of the city caught sight of all of the images of the gods lying on the ground, he came to worship Mary and the infant Jesus, and all his people were converted to Christ's teaching when they saw the wonder which had come to pass.

Another legend tells us that in a great city to which they came there was "a god image to which the other images and gods made gifts and devotions. And by the image was an attendant priest, who, as soon as Satan spoke from the image, informed the inhabitants and districts of Egypt of his words." So far the legend is right, since there often were speaking-oracle statues in Egyptian temples. This might be managed by placing the image of the god on a hollow podium, with a speaking tube leading down to a secret underground room, from which a priest pronounced the oracle's words. Such magic apparatuses have been unearthed by excavations. "Now when Jesus and Mary came to the city . . . the inhabitants became very disturbed, and all the officials and priests came to the image of the oracle and asked, 'What is this confusion and consternation which has gripped our land?' And the oracle answered them, saying, 'An unknown god has come here. He is the true god and other than he, no other god is worthy of divine worship, for he is the true son of God. It was at this news that the land trembled, and upon his arrival, became disturbed and disconcerted. We too have great fear of his mighty kingdom.' And at that moment, the image of the god toppled over, and at its fall, all the inhabitants of Egypt ran to each other."

Here the oracle of the highest pagan god, meeting the infant Jesus in Egypt, is allowed to prophesy what actually happened a few hundred years later, when the Christians moved from one heathen temple to the next, smashing the images of the gods, defying all the magic of the pagans—in which the Christians also believed but which they had the holy strength to overcome.

The infant Jesus—sometimes only his diaper—heals the sick and cures the afflicted. Even one who has been turned into a donkey by magic, he turns back into a man, certainly a difficult feat. Many places became holy because of the infant Jesus' visit. Outside Cairo, in the little village of Matarie, they still point out today a sycamore tree, in the shade of which Mary and the infant supposedly rested. To be sure, the present tree was planted in the year 1672, but the much older legend indicates that it replaced another sycamore which stood on the spot earlier. There is also a spring in Matarie which Jesus is supposed to have summoned forth, so that Mary might wash his baby clothes. When she did so, the water took on a balsamic fragrance.

Finally the holy family reached the ancient capital of Memphis, just south of Cairo. "When they had seen Pharaoh," the collection of legends concludes, "they stayed for three years in Egypt, and Jesus accomplished many other wonders in Egypt, which are not written down in the childhood evangel [as the collection of legends is called] or in the complete evangel."

Jesus' stay in Egypt could also be used in a manner quite different from its treatment in these legends, often simpleminded, but just as often touching and beautiful, intended for the edification of Egyptian Christians. Since ancient times Egypt had the reputation of being the land of magicians, and not even the Christian biographies of saints deny that the pagan priests had great magic powers which could only be bested by the holiest of men. This aspect was seized upon by anti-Christian propaganda.

According to a Jewish tradition, directed against Christianity, Jesus was a magician, born out of wedlock, and his mother, Mary, had to flee to Egypt with her lover, Joseph, in order to avoid being stoned to death according to Herod's righteous judgment. This tradition goes back as far as the second century after Christ. It was in Egypt that he learned his magic arts, it was said, and the wonders wrought by Jesus in Egypt could be used to support this view. A wise man, Elieser ben Hyrkanos, who had personal contacts with one of Jesus' disciples and had therefore fallen into disfavor with the more orthodox, is supposed to have recounted that Jesus had tattooed on his body the magic formulas which he had learned in Egypt. In this way he had taken them back with him to Palestine in order to lead the people astray. When a disciple asked what should be said of something like tattooing oneself with magic formulas, he got the answer that it was only Ben Stada (a Jewish name for Jesus) who had done this, and he, of course, was a madman.

Since it would still have been evidence of something supernatural that a newborn child should be able to learn magic, another tradition tells us that Jesus grew up in obscurity and worked as a day laborer in Egypt. There he practiced his magical arts in order to return home and present himself as a god, with their help. According to one Jewish tradition, it was also in his capacity as a magician that Jesus was executed. The crowning event was when he stole god's unpronounceable name from the temple. With the help of this, he could soar in the air—to his own terror, initially—until Judas managed to steal the holy name from him as he slept.

And so we see that the evangel's simple story of the flight into Egypt could just as well be used in the sharpest attacks on Christianity as in the garland of oriental legends, which for thousands of years have inspired artists of the Christian West to create irreplaceable masterpieces.

Coptic

In the 1930s a philologist was engaged in the study of various dialects in Upper Egypt. In a small, out-of-the-way village he encountered a few older men who spoke a unique language, incomprehensible to their neighbors. Malice has it that it was used, among other things, as a secret language in not quite legal activities, but this may be doing the old villagers an injustice. It was Coptic they were speaking, a language which was thought to have died out as a spoken language hundreds of years earlier. To be sure, Coptic was still being used in the Christian churches in Egypt, but as a dead language, its pronunciation wholly conventionalized and based on no living tradition. A few members of the Coptic church had tried to bring the language back to life, as has now been done with Hebrew in Israel, but they had made very little headway.

Now one had finally found a living Coptic tradition, and the old peasants were subjected to a thorough inquisition by scholars. They had to recite texts which they knew from memory, and their pronunciation was carefully noted. The old peasants themselves could not at all understand this interest in their uneducated pronunciation. Why, in church you could hear a much

283

better and more proper pronunciation, they pointed out. As soon as the philologists asked them detailed questions about a particular pronunciation, they took it as a criticism and immediately fell in with the conventional church pronunciation. The interesting thing was that the speech of the old peasants reflected the ancient language in a richer and often truer sense, and their pronunciation supplied answers to a number of problems of linguistic history. From the mouths of these old peasants, one heard the last living echo of that language which had been the country's own from Egypt's age of glory under the Pharaohs all the way up to the end of the first millennium after Christ, when the majority of the population had gone over to Islam and to speaking Arabic, which is now the official language of Egypt.

What is most interesting about Coptic is that it permits us some approach to the pronunciation of the ancient Egyptian language. In many ways, Coptic became the means by which one could resurrect knowledge of this completely dead and forgotten language.

Coptic had been brought into being by purely practical requirements. Ancient Egyptian was written in hieroglyphics, and this writing only reproduced the consonants. The vowels did not have to be written out, since one who knew the language could still read the words correctly because of the character of the writing. The system was rather as though we were to write the letters *b r d* and then draw a loaf of bread, when the word was to read *bread*, and a bird, when the word was to read *bird*. Someone who knew the language had no trouble with the pronunciation, but we moderns, who cannot speak it, have to sit and mumble as well as we can without vowels. The script developed into a very difficult cursive style, which only a scholar could handle, and when Egypt became Christian, during the second century after Christ, and the Bible was to be translated into Egyptian, a more readable script was required. And so a new system of writing Egyptian was developed. It was written with Greek letters, including the vowels. For some sounds which did not exist in Greek, symbols from the ancient native script were used. This Coptic system of writing, in other words, is the first one to reproduce the Egyptian vowels, and it reflects approximately the language spoken at the beginning of the Christian era. What we call Coptic is really only a later stage of development of the ancient Egyptian.

Coptic is the final stage of a very long development which we can trace through thousands of years, and there is just as great a difference between the earliest Egyptian we know (from about 3000 B.C.) and Coptic, as there is between the earliest Latin and Parisian slang, to take a modern parallel.

Coptic is not a uniform language. Even in the earliest writings, and there particularly, we find a number of different local dialects. Now it is fortunate that the various dialects have preserved earlier features in different ways, so that with the help of the dialects, we can figure out the original old Egyptian form. Behind these reconstructions lie long and complicated labors of scholarship, and we have still not got so far as to work out the pronunciation of all the early words.

What Coptic reflects was not exactly a high point of Egyptian culture or language development, and it is actually a rather poor language. As is often the case with a language in this condition, it abounds with borrowed words. In a normal Coptic text approximately thirty per cent of the words have been borrowed from Greek, and this seems to have been something of a fashion. Often it was done even when a Coptic word existed. Moreover, Coptic did not lack possibilities for building new words. On the contrary, the construction of the language made this quite easy.

I shall not try to give any language lessons in Coptic, but it may be worth while to give some indications of how the language is constructed.

Most characteristic, perhaps, is the Coptic manner of combining a large number of more or less unchanging words elements into a giant word, which is pronounced as a single connected word with an accented main syllable. To take apart such word monsters can often be rather difficult for a beginner, and the whole thing is not made any easier by the fact that the Coptic script does not separate the words from one another, but simply runs each complete concept together as one connected word. Long words on the order of antidisestablishmentarianism are the usual means of expressing all the related elements of a concept. To be God-fearing, for example, is expressed in Coptic as *mntrefshemshenute*, which is a combination of *mnt* ("thing," a particle which is used to build abstract substantives), *ref* ("man who does"), *shemshe* ("serve"), and *nute* ("God").

Even entire phrases can be expressed by a single word. If, for example, you want to say in Coptic "that you are God-fearing," it would be *djentetnhenrefshemshenute*, literally: *dje* ("that") *ntetn* ("you"), *hen* (indefinite article, actually "something of"), and then *ref* ("man who does"), *shemshe* ("serve"), *nute* ("God"). The same predilection for combinations is typical of large parts of the grammar, and the great majority of the verb forms are constructed with auxiliary verbs which mean "be" or "do." In Coptic one does not say "I do" but "I do do," not "I did" (i.e., the bent form) but "I was doing."

Coptic is not only interesting as a late descendant of the Pharaoh's language, it has enriched our knowledge of times past in other ways as well.

The Coptic texts which survived to our own day were primarily texts from the Bible and other common Christian texts, such as sermons, biographies of saints, and rules for conducting services, but these were most often translations from Greek or Syrian. More original texts concern the earliest monasticism, which developed in Egypt, and there was one man in particular, the monastic leader Shenute, who created a national literature of importance. Then there are a large number of letters, tax receipts, and business records which give us some insights into daily life in Egypt during the first millennium of the Christian era.

The most interesting thing the Coptic texts have to offer, however, is something quite different and much more sensational.

The earliest Christian church had a number of competitors in other, often rather similar religions, and the most dangerous competition came from the various Gnostic "heresies." Gnosticism is a modern collective term for an incalculable number of such "erroneous teachings," and it is difficult to give a short definition of what they had in common. Characteristic is the conception of God as the Creator of all things, infinitely raised above his creation and separated from it by a great number of divine beings, aeons, of lesser quality the farther they stand from the Creator. The last and lowest of the aeons was the demi-urge, who created this world, and was often identified with the Old Testament Jahve. Man, who lives on earth, is a combination of both divine and material elements, and his divine element, his soul, longs to free itself from the prison of the material and to return to its divine origin. To attain this salvation, man must achieve insight into his true situation, and knowledge "gnosis"—of this comes to him through a savior, often identified with Jesus, who descends from the world of divine light into the darkness in which the soul lies captive.

The points of similarity to Christianity are many, and several sects had begun with precisely the Christian teaching as the starting point for their speculations. Others were based on pagan beliefs, and still others, like the Manichaeans, made a synthesis of the various religions of the time in order to create from them a new universal religion, intended primarily for the universal realm which the Persians, in the 200s, dreamed of raising in competition with the Romans.

Gnosticism was both a popular movement and a development which appealed to the most gifted thinkers of the time. We might recall, for example, that Augustine in his youth embraced the Manichaean doctrine. This was therefore a genuinely dangerous opponent for the Christian church, which had great trouble remaining untainted by Gnosticism and maintaining its position of religio-political power. The struggle was waged not only with the sword of the spirit; the ultimate victory of the church was probably in many respects just as much a victory of brute strength.

The result was a grim persecution of the Gnostics, and their writings were destroyed. But ideas have an uncanny gift for surviving persecution. For a long time knowledge of the Gnostic beliefs had to be built primarily on what their enemies, the Christian church fathers, had to say about them, and these references were presumably colored by polemic intensity. Here new finds of Coptic texts have completely altered the picture.

The first one was made in the year 1930, when a rather large collection of original Manichaean texts was found in Coptic translations. As yet, only some of them have been studied scientifically and published. They were in very poor condition and tried the patience of experts to the utmost. As though this were not enough, their earlier misfortunes seem to pursue them even in modern times. Part of the find went to England, where it is now safely preserved, but the rest was taken to Berlin. The majority of the writings fell into Russian hands during the war and, for the time being at least, are no longer accessible to specialists studying the texts. The parts published so far have thrown new light on the Manichaean religion, of which we now finally have a firmer understanding. Particularly fascinating is the collection of Manichaean psalms, which even in their Coptic dress give some suggestion of the poetic beauty which captivated a man like the young Augustine. Moreover, they provided solutions to some of the problems connected with the relationship between Manichaeism and another important Gnostic religion, Mandaeism—a teaching which we still find today among a group of peasants in Iraq.

The second great find of Gnostic texts attracted still more attention. This discovery was made in 1945, by some Egyptian peasants, near Nag Hammadi, in Upper Egypt. They had no real conception of the value of the find and sold it for the modest price of about twelve dollars. Seldom has so poor a business deal been concluded in the Nile Valley.

Through unfathomable channels one of these writings found its way to Cairo the next year and was purchased by the Coptic museum. It was a book bound in leather, one of the earliest known bindings, and closer study revealed that it contained no fewer than five original Gnostic works in Coptic, or, more precisely, in Coptic translation.

The first book was followed by others. In the antique trade a private person managed to get hold of another one. The expert who finally had a chance to look at it soon determined that here were texts which could be ascribed to Valentinus, a Gnostic from the middle of the second century. He had originally belonged to the Christian church, but after a vain attempt in Rome to be made a bishop, he broke with the church and built his own sect, one of the church's most formidable opponents. This important book disappeared once again from Cairo, and only after long, roundabout travels, it popped up again in Brussels, where it was purchased by the Swiss Jung Institute. A not insignificant background to the book's curious fate during recent years is the fact that export of such texts is forbidden by Egyptian law.

In the meantime, a private person had quietly managed to buy up the rest of the peasants' find of handwritten texts. In 1949 he turned to the Coptic museum in Cairo and started to negotiate their sale. Now it was no longer a question of a price in two figures, but there were rumors that sums of around a million dollars were discussed. The end of the matter was that the state seized the writings, and the legal question of compensation for the owner has apparently not yet been settled.

An international committee has been formed for scholarly study and publication of the texts. In the meantime, the Egyptians have begun to publish photographic reproductions of the various books. In toto, the collection consists of eleven books, of which nine are well preserved.

The first volume to be purchased has still not been published, but the contents are partially known, because a couple of the texts also appear in a handwritten text which the Berlin Museum has owned for some time but which was not published until 1955. That part of the Jung Institute's text which contains "Truth's Evangel," or, rather, a baptismal sermon by Valentinus, was published in 1956. Last year the first part of the Egyptian facsimile edition of the latest acquisitions was made available for reading by those who know Coptic. The large circle of experts who are fascinated by the riddles and problems of Gnosticism now have their hands full, and specialists in Coptic, not too numerous, have assumed a more important role as interpreters of texts for theologians and religious historians than they ever dreamed of. Coptic has become the key language for anyone who intends to study the conflicts of faith during the second and third centuries, a time of decisive importance in the formation of the Christian church.

The significance of these new Coptic texts can be illustrated with an example, and we might then choose the now much-debated question of whether women can be ministers. Practically everyone assumes that the only texts which can have any importance are the canonical texts, the texts which can be read in our ordinary Bible. This means that either in innocent ignorance or in conscious acceptance of the church's orthodox conception, one approves the choices of tradition which the church made during the first centuries after Christ and definitively established as canon in the 300s. But alongside the canonical tradition of Jesus' life and words, which we find in the four evangels, there is a rich growth of other evangels and similar texts. In part, the selections were made just at the time of the vigorous struggles with Gnosticism, and it is not unreasonable to assume that this circumstance affected the choices made.

The evangel of John seems to have been written for a public familiar with Gnosticism. This is indicated, among other things, by the choice of words in the prologue, which takes on full meaning only when seen in the light of Gnostic thinking. But the church would go no further. A number of evangels about Jesus were purely Gnostic and were therefore thrown out. Others came into disrepute not because of their contents, but because they were particularly cherished by the church's Gnostic opponents.

One such evangel, which in terms of content could hardly have disturbed even the most orthodox but which was still eliminated, appears in its entirety in the newly published Egyptian facsimile edition. No translation has yet been published. Here it is called the evangel of Thomas, and we know that the Manichaeans, among the church's arch-enemies, used it sedulously. From citations by the church fathers, it appears originally to have been called the Hebrew evangel and to have been written for Jewish Christians.

It contains a collection of Jesus' sayings, for the most part variations of the parables and pronouncements which can be read particularly in the evangels of Luke and Matthew. A few Greek fragments of this text were known earlier from papyri from the Egyptian city of Oxyrhynchus, and attracted great attention when they first appeared.

There is no real historical reason why this text should not contain just as old and reliable a tradition as the canonical evangels. It is pretty well accepted that the Matthew and Luke evangels were based on, among other things, a traditional collection of Jesus' "speeches" and sayings, the so-called "speech source," or Logia source, and so far as I can see, we have every reason to assume that the Thomas evangel or Hebrew evangel is a version of this, independent of the canonical evangels.

In discussions about Jesus' conception of one thing or another, a text like the Thomas evangel should therefore not be excluded. If one believes in the canonical evangels, there is no reason to discard *a priori* this independent tradition. If you are not willing to accept this also, you might as well leave the

Bible out of the discussion and be completely guided by your own ideas and what conditions today call for—an attitude which does not lack spokesmen either.

The Thomas evangel concludes with the following notable passage which may have a certain current significance:

"Simon Petrus said to them: 'Let Mary leave us, for women are not worthy [of eternal] life.'"

"Jesus said: 'Behold, I shall carry her up to me, for I shall make her a man, so that she herself may become a living spirit, like unto your men. For every woman, who is made a man, shall enter the kingdom of heaven.'"

This saying follows about the same line as Paul's often-cited "Here is neither man nor woman" and Luke's "They which shall be accounted worthy to obtain that world, and the resurrection from the dead, neither marry, nor are given in marriage." In other words, from the standpoint of salvation, the sexes are unimportant, and the Saviour can make woman the equal of man.

The church's emphasis on the special status of man is perhaps partially the product of the struggle with the Gnostics. For the latter, the sexes belonged to the material, the opposite of the spiritual. Both men and women had to free themselves from this in order to have any hope of salvation, and therefore the woman was no less suited than the man to help herself and others to salvation.

This was put forth very strongly in a number of purely Gnostic evangels, in which Mary or Mary Magdalene often occupies an important position as the one who presents the true teaching of Jesus to the disciples. This role of woman in the holy texts of its opponents may have strengthened the church's emphasis on the masculine. It is typical that the one among the disciples who reacts most strongly against women, in the Gnostic evangels, as in the Thomas evangel, is Peter, of whom Jesus said: "Thou art Peter, and on this rock shall I build my church."

This contrasting view is formulated most drastically, perhaps, in the so-called Mary evangel, preserved in the Coptic-Gnostic text in Berlin, published in 1955, which was probably composed no later than the second century.

After the death of Jesus the disciples are deliberating about what they should actually preach, and in their dilemma they turn to Mary Magdalene.

"We know that the Saviour loved you more than other women. Tell us then the words of the Saviour which you remember but we do not, and which we have not heard."

Mary gives them a long, purely Gnostic rendering, which shocks the disciples. Peter in particular reacts strongly:

"Would he really have spoken with a woman, unbeknownst to us? Should we turn around and listen to her? Would he really have addressed her before us?"

Mary begins to cry and answers: "My brother Peter, what do you believe anyway? Do you think that I have invented this myself or that I am lying about the Saviour?"

Then Levi intercedes like a gentleman and says to Peter: "Peter, you have always been a man quick to anger. Now I see that you also excite yourself against a woman. If the Saviour considered her worthy, who then are you to reject her?"

Scoundrel or saint:
the Coptic monk Shenute

When the Christian church had managed, by various means, to render more or less harmless its most dangerous competitors, the different Gnostic sects, there still followed no period of peace. The external struggles were succeeded by conflicts within the church, and in the 400s after Christ this had gone so far that the churches of the Orient and of the West had gone their separate ways because, among other things, they could not agree about the problem of Christ—whether Christ was man and god, or, as was maintained in the Orient, solely god, who only seemingly appeared as a man. It was also at this time that the Christians in Egypt created their own congregation, the Coptic church, which was separate from both the Greek Orthodox and the Catholic.

Behind the battles over dogma there was also a struggle for power among the leading men of the church—above all, among the archbishops in the three great cities in the East—Alexandria in Egypt, Antioch in Syria, and Constantinople.

In the year 431 a council of the church had been convoked in the city of Ephesus in order to judge Nestorius, the archbishop of Antioch, for his erroneous teachings. Nestorius arrived with armed troops, significant enough for the time. Also Cyril, Alexandria's archbishop, had provided himself with a bodyguard, and, among others, he had with him a big and strong Coptic monk named Shenute, who, according to his own account, played a lively part in the discussions.

It is a disciple of this Shenute who tells us that when the church fathers had entered the church and seated themselves on their thrones, still another throne was set up, on which the holy gospels were placed, as though they, too, should participate in the deliberations. The villain of the drama, Archbishop Nestorius, came too late, and there was no place left for him. When he entered, as we hear, "with arrogant and shameless pomp and state," he lifted down the holy gospels and seated himself on the throne. "When my father Shenute saw what Nestorius had done, he immediately leapt up in righteous rage among our holy fathers, picked up the holy gospels from the floor, and struck the impious Nestorius right on the chest, and said: 'Do you wish God's son to sit on the floor, while you yourself sit on a throne?' "

"What is your business here, who are neither bishop nor church leader, but only a monk?" Nestorius managed to stammer forth. But then "he fell from the throne and became like a demon amid the congregation of our fathers."

After having delivered this and other striking arguments in the church controversy, Shenute was to return home to Egypt. But when he came down to the boat, the sailors said to him: "You cannot travel with the archbishop!" "You see, they did not recognize Shenute," says the pious narrator, "because his appearance was always so simple and he conducted himself with such humility." Shenute did not protest, but went off by himself and prayed to our Lord, who immediately had a luminous cloud bear him and his disciples to the monastery in Egypt. And when the bishops arrived in Egypt after the hard sea journey, Shenute was home and had already had time to accomplish still another miracle.

He had put a kernel of grain, which he had found in Ephesus, in one of the monastery's mills, and through one of God's miracles, an unheard-of quantity of flour poured from the mill. The brothers labored without stopping for three days and three nights and filled storehouse after storehouse, but at last it was too much of a good thing. The brothers began to grumble, but no matter how they tried, they could not stop the mill. Then finally Shenute laid his staff upon it and said: "I say to you, millstone, stop!" And it halted immediately.

Who, then, is this remarkable monk, who strikes the church fathers senseless, who flies home from the church council on a luminous cloud, and who has the power to work wonders? He must have been an important man, to be the subject of such a rich body of legend and to become one of the holiest men of the Coptic church.

We know him rather well. One of his disciples has written a long account of him, but here he has already become an idealized saint figure, which has little to do with the real Shenute. However, we also have his own writings, letters, and sermons, which flowed from his pen in endless quantities. Through them, we learn a great deal both about him and about the conditions in Egypt in his time.

It is both a fascinating and a disheartening vista which unrolls before our eyes.

Ever since the Romans had conquered Egypt in the year 31 B.C., the land had been regarded primarily as a source of taxes, which one sucked dry to the best of one's ability. Now and then there were revolts, but the broad mass of the people almost never had anything to gain from this. In the battles the peasants had their fields destroyed, and the new regime almost always levied a few more taxes to restore finances after the war. For the peasants and for the people in general, it was much the same whoever ruled the country.

The land had to a great extent passed over either into the hands of the crown or of the great landowners, and it was worked by day laborers. These poor wretches were shamelessly exploited. They were badly paid, and to top it all off, they were often not even given their pay. The landowners were hard masters, and once when Shenute threatened them with all the tortures of hell if they did not conduct themselves better toward their inferiors, they laughed and said: "Hell is probably overcrowded already, so there will not be any room for us." But Shenute assured them that when they had been burned to ashes, they and many more would find room there.

The government administered the land badly. The irrigation system was mismanaged, the crops failed, and famine raged. When the income from taxes was reduced as a result, the taxes were only raised still more, and extorted by the rawest means. The soldiers often went without their pay, but they made up their losses by plundering and ravaging the land. A contemporary tells us: "Villages and cities, houses, roads and ships, gardens, fields, harvests, grain stores and monasteries, yes, even offerings brought forward in the house of God, are plundered by the soldiers. If anyone protests, they place a knife at his throat and threaten his life. Many they mistreat and tie to the torture stake, and their acts of violence are like those of the barbarians."

Barbarians, yes—in Upper Egypt another curse wracked the land. Nubian tribes constantly broke in across the southern border and ravaged the countryside. Tens of thousands of people fled from them in panic and sought refuge in the fortified cloisters which could hold out against attacks, but just as many fell victim to the plundering hordes. "Great numbers of people drowned in the river, many died up in the desert mountains, many were carried off as prisoners, many virgins were ravished, churches were burned down or plundered," recounts an eyewitness.

Under these terrifying conditions in the land, there were many who sought escape from the world and lived as hermits in the desert. Some of these hermits gathered a flock of disciples around them, and so the first monasteries came into existence, the first in the history of the Christian church. This new way of life spread quickly throughout Egypt, but monasticism owed its first real boom to the monk Shenute.

He was the son of a poor, landowning peasant and as a boy had been sent to his uncle Pgol's monastery. Since he was energetic and intelligent, he was soon permitted to help with the administration of the monastery, and when Pgol died, Shenute succeeded him. Under his leadership the monastery flourished, and the number of monks grew from tens to thousands and ten thousands. Shenute's power became ever greater. Nunneries also came under his control, and hermits in the regions were forced to subordinate themselves to the monastery.

Those who sought their way into the monasteries were certainly not always the best children of God. It was probably not always as much a warm Christian faith as it was the hopeless social and economic conditions in the land which caused the fantastic growth of the monasteries. From Shenute himself we learn that many became monks only to get a secure livelihood in the monasteries and to escape the relentless economic difficulties. Others who were skilled craftsmen felt that the free market was too troublesome, with its taxes and regulations, and became monks simply in order to work in peace and quiet. Still others, who had no trade, entered the monastery to receive free training, and later left it again.

When you see how the monks and the nuns lived, you can understand how terrible life must have been in Egypt at the time, if anyone entered cloisters with such motives and not because of a firm faith.

On entering a monastery one was forced to dispose of all one's earthly possessions, preferably to the monastery, of course, but this was not required. Within the monastery all were equal, all wore the same habits, and all ate the same food. The habit had to be worn until it fell apart. No ostentation was permitted, and the monks were even forbidden to bathe, to wash their heads or feet, or to comb their hair with any special care.

Food was served only once a day, and no matter how bad it might be, one might not disdain it—it was all a gift from God. As a rule, only bread was served; once a week there were cooked vegetables. The drink was water, but even of this one was not allowed to drink more than was absolutely necessary— in any case, never two full cups one right after the other. It was strictly forbidden to consume anything except at this single meal, which was served in the evening. Only the sick received extra food, and it is not surprising that many should have pretended to be sick to get a few days of sweet bread.

The main thing in the monastery was not, as one might expect, quiet meditation, but instead hard work from morning to night. Preferably, the work was to be disagreeable and tedious. "He who does not work, does not eat" was a basic premise acted upon to the utmost degree.

A few tried to get away with something by constantly interrupting their work to kneel and pray. Strong regulations were therefore enacted, specifying how many prayer sessions and prayers were allowed. When a bell was rung, everyone had immediately to kneel and pray, but one was to get it over with quickly. Shenute established a formal regimen for kneeling and praying, and at the services, when several priests were to read aloud, one after another, number two was to stand in readiness even before number one had finished, so that no time should be wasted.

For the poor monks, semi-starvation and slave labor were not enough. Over them stood Shenute like an avenging angel. He saw to it that the strict—yes, one can rightly say, inhuman— monastery regulations were observed down to the last detail. The slightest transgression was punished with the utmost severity, generally by flogging, and in the monastery it was Shenute himself who delivered the punishment.

He was greatly disturbed because an abbess would not permit him also to chastise the nuns when necessary. On occasion he had done so, and as he himself writes in a letter, "The whole town echoed with the pitiful cries and lamentations of the sisters." After this experience Shenute had to be content to issue detailed written instruction regarding the punishments. There are long lists:

"Theonoe, Apa Hermef's daughter, who transgressed grievously and stole: 30 raps of the cane."

"Sophia, who you have told me stubbornly contradicted her teacher and many others without reason, and who gave the abbess a blow on the ear: 20 raps of the cane."

"Taese, little Pshai's sister, who hastened to Sansno filled with bodily lust: 15 raps of the cane."

"Your sister Apolle also deserves some raps of the cane. But for the sake of God and for our own, we shall forgive her this time—I know that she could not bear the raps of the cane, since she is so big and fat."

A monk was dispatched to deliver the canings, and the abbess and the older nuns were to hold the delinquent. If the poor nun made opposition, Shenute was to be notified, and he would then threaten to take part himself.

This threat was probably more frightening than any other. Shenute was a violent man and extremely strong. He struck hard in moods of anger, and at best the monks were carried away senseless. On one occasion he actually killed a monk. At first Shenute was very contrite and wrote a letter to the brothers to beg forgiveness. But before the letter was finished, he had begun to think differently: If the monk he had punished had not sinned so greatly, Shenute would not have been driven to commit his own sin. In other words, the whole thing was the wretched monk's fault, who not only sinned himself, but who also caused others to sin!

No doubt the monks often grumbled against this hard regime, but mostly when Shenute was away. Then they might write him complaining letters, but as soon as he returned, no one dared to oppose him.

Through this strict organization, and because the monasteries were run almost like industrial enterprises, Shenute became a really powerful figure in the whole of Upper Egypt. Toward everyone he acted as inconsiderately and violently as a dictator. Within the monastery his rule was absolute, and soon he laid claim to the same power even outside the monastery walls. More than one Christian in the area had to pay with his life for not heeding Shenute's exhortations to penance. Shenute's punishments were regarded by the people as judgments of God. As a rule, no one dared to protest, even when Shenute committed murder, openly or in secret.

One father had placed his poor son in the monastery, but the boy was not happy there and committed the sin of asking to be allowed to return home. Shenute replied that he should certainly be permitted to return to his father. The same day the boy fell ill. Shenute refused to care for him, and soon the boy went home to his father—in heaven, as the pious story tells us.

Another time Shenute openly murdered a man and a woman living in sin. He was charged with murder, and his defense was the fact that King Samuel had killed Agag, the king of the Amalekites, so why should not he, Shenute, be allowed to do as Samuel did, when he punished sin? This was of no help. Shenute was condemned to die. The executioner's sword was already raised, the chronicle tells us, when two angels came down from heaven and rescued Shenute. We need hardly doubt that the monks were the ones who delivered their feared but beloved leader from the hands of justice.

In the same way, Shenute managed to save himself on yet another occasion, when he had attacked a pagan temple. There were still quite a few heathens in the land, and Shenute's very special wrath was directed against them and their temples. We are told, for example, that some pagan vineyard owners had sold sour wine to the Christians and that Shenute pronounced such a terrible curse upon the island on which the vineyards stood that it sank into the Nile. Another time a pagan was careless enough to deal Shenute a blow on the ear. "But then,"

we learn, "someone came"—and it was certainly Shenute himself—"and seized the impious one by the hair, gave him a slap
on the ear, and dragged him through the entire city. And a
great crowd followed after, until he came to the river, where
he threw him into the water. Since then [the wretched pagan]
has never been seen again."

Pagan temple after pagan temple was plundered and destroyed by Shenute, eagerly supported by the monks and the
Christian mobs. Expensive goods found in the sacred shrines
were placed in the monastery coffers, and the stones of the
ruined temples were used to build additions to the cloisters,
which grew larger and larger.

Once Shenute was officially charged with one of these assaults. The judge was a pagan, and the city in which judgment
was to be pronounced was mainly populated by pagans. But
Shenute did not find himself alone. From all the Christian
towns and cities streamed great troops of people, more and
more of them, so that all the streets and squares were filled.
When the trial was to begin, they shouted as one man, "Jesus!
Jesus!" with such force that the judge could not make himself
heard. The trial had to be called off, and Shenute was conducted in triumph to the church, where he preached a glowing
sermon on the pagans' punishment to come.

How, then, could it happen that so many—in blind obedience
and with burning enthusiasm—followed such a man, whose
path, according to any normal earthly judgment, was marked
by slashes and blows, theft and murder?

The reasons were several. He was a divinely inspired speaker
and preacher. Like fire, his words burned their marks on men's
minds—words which frightened but fascinated. Anyone who
once came within his magic circle could never be free again.
For centuries afterward, his words would be regarded as the
highest models, second only to the Holy Scriptures, and he
created a Coptic national literature.

Under his leadership the monasteries acquired such a position
that they could really be secure, if somewhat uncomfortable,

harbors in a singularly evil world. Not only those who were monks or nuns could derive benefits from this. When there was famine, the monastery doled out food to the starving, and when the wild, plundering Nubian hordes swept through the land, tens of thousands of people could find refuge behind the strong monastery walls. With the rich, Shenute used both hell-fire sermons and ingratiating words to induce them to help the poor.

Although many had bitter cause to hate Shenute, there were many more who had him to thank for their lives. He was one part scoundrel, with blood on his hands; the other part saint, a miraculous savior in time of need.

Through Shenute's work the Coptic church acquired its distinct character; from him, it derived its inner strength. This church still remains in Egypt today. Islam has squeezed it out from its former dominance, but still it is the Coptic church in Egypt which appoints the head of the Christian church in Abyssinia. The effects of the lifework of the remarkable monk Shenute still live on.

And all the Christian monk orders in the world can ultimately be traced back to these first important monasteries in Egypt, during that land's deepest decay.

INDEX

Index

Italicized page numbers refer to illustrations.